The Acquisition of Language

The Acquisition of Language

Second Edition

Helen Smith Cairns

pro·ed

8700 Shoal Creek Boulevard
Austin, Texas 78757-6897

pro·ed

© 1996, 1986 by PRO-ED, Inc.
8700 Shoal Creek Boulevard
Austin, Texas 78757-6897

The PRO-ED **Studies in Communicative Disorders** series
Series Editor: Harvey Halpern

Library of Congress Cataloging-in-Publication Data

Cairns, Helen Smith.
    The acquisition of language / Helen Smith Cairns. — [2nd ed.]
        p.   cm. — (PRO-ED studies in communicative disorders)
    Includes bibliographical references (p.) and index.
    ISBN 0-89079-672-6 (pbk.)
    1. Language acquisition. I. Title. II. Series.
P118.C34 1995   95-17365
401′ .93—dc20   CIP

This book is designed in Eras and Trump Medieval.

Production Manager: Alan Grimes
Production Coordinator: Karen Swain
Managing Editor: Tracy Sergo
Designer: Thomas Barkley
Reprints Buyer: Alicia Woods
Editor: Debra Berman
Editorial Assistant: Claudette Landry

Printed in the United States of America

2 3 4 5 6 7 8 9 10   00 99 98 97 96

This work is dedicated to my grandchildren:

Jonathan Joseph Stafford
Daniel Richard Stafford
Joseph George Stafford
Nicholas John Stafford
and
Hannah Grace Eunhwa Suh

who are in five different stages of language acquisition

Contents

Preface

This book is intended for students or professionals in a wide variety of disciplines—speech–language pathology, psychology, linguistics, or education—who want a basic introduction to the field of developmental psycholinguistics. My goal is to capture the richness of this complex field, yet present the information in such a way that no prior knowledge of psychology or linguistics is required.

Last year the Public Broadcasting System presented a series entitled *A Glorious Accident*, in which they involved a number of scientists and philosophers in discussions of the nature of mind and consciousness. Stephen Jay Gould, the Harvard paleontologist, astutely observed that science cannot answer such large questions; it can only address individual, empirically tractable issues that relate to the larger ones. The nature–nurture debate, which has consumed philosophy, psychology, and individual intellects for generations, is an issue of similar scope. To what extent is a person shaped by biological factors and to what extent by individual experience? Modern linguistics and developmental psycholinguistics allow us to approach this large question scientifically in the empirically tractable domain of language and language development. We now see the phenomenon of human language and its acquisition as a special case of the close linkage between nature and nurture. The interaction of uniquely human properties of the neurological system and exposure to natural language produces a system of knowledge and behavior that virtually defines our species.

The theoretical framework adopted in this book is nativist in that language acquisition is seen as the product of an interaction between "innate," biological characteristics of infants and children, and their experience with the speech of their environment. Modern linguistic theory provides some specific proposals regarding what properties of language may be part of our evolutionary heritage; the theoretical framework adopted here is generally known as the "Principles and Parameters" approach. However, linguistic theory, like all rich, dynamic theories, is constantly changing and evolving. The research reported in this book and the advances observed in developmental psycholinguistics do not depend on the details of any particular linguistic theory. Developmental psycholinguistics, while guided by theoretical linguistics, is an independent field with its own trajectory. Good empirical research, while necessarily informed by theory, transcends particular narrow theoretical formulations. This kind of empirical research is the focus of this book.

In authoring a work of such brevity, one must choose between depth and breadth. I have opted for the former. Many important aspects of child language, such as phonological development, are virtually ignored. Another book in this PRO-ED series, *Language Disorders of Children*, by Richard Schwartz (in press), gives a full account of that aspect of language development. Other important areas, such as pragmatics and discourse, are touched on only lightly in this book. A great deal of good work has been done in this area recently, and many excellent secondary sources exist, such as Foster (1990), Gallagher (1991), Nelson (1986), and Ochs and Schiefflin (1979). There seemed to be a real need, however, for a comprehensive (though certainly not exhaustive) review of research in the acquisition of syntax and vocabulary, the building blocks of the sentence, which, in turn, is the basic unit of all discourse. Neither have I attempted to provide anything like a formal introduction to linguistic theory. Atkinson (1992) and Goodluck (1991) have both written such books, presenting acquisition within a full account of contemporary theory. Instead, I have chosen to concentrate on empirical findings, providing just enough theoretical machinery to make the research comprehensible. There is the danger, in an attempt to make the research seem cohesive, that I might have made everything appear too neat. There is probably not a single conclusion presented in the entire text that would not be called into question by someone, somewhere. I have tried, however, to represent fairly mainstream points of view and to provide the reader with the tools to think intelligently about the issues and assess different points of view when they are encountered.

The book is organized in the following way. The first chapter discusses some of the general properties of human language that have crucial entailments for language development. Chapter 2 presents the theoretical framework adopted by the book. Chapter 3 provides an overview of the sequence of language development, concentrating on production in the early years. Chapter 4 reviews much current work on acquisition of syntax, and Chapter 5 addresses a variety of topics in lexical learning. Chapter 6 is the only chapter that goes beyond sentence-level processes. It touches on pragmatic and communicative development but addresses fairly extensively the acquisition of metalinguistic skills and the relationship of all aspects of language development to early reading.

I have chosen to deal with the notorious gender referral problem by alternating pronoun genders in the six chapters. Thus, the child is "she" in Chapter 1, "he" in Chapter 2, and so on.

A number of people have been generous in their assistance during various stages of the production of this book. I have profited greatly from conversations with Chuck Cairns, Jennifer Ryan Hsu, and Janine Graziano-King. Phil Connell and Dana McDaniel have each read the entire manuscript and provided helpful comments. I am also deeply appreciative to the students in my Spring 1994 graduate seminar in acquisition of syntax at the City University of New York for helping me think through many important theoretical and empirical issues. My colleague and friend, the series editor, Harvey Halpern, has always provided welcome assistance and encouragement. My thanks to all these folk, along with apologies for any remaining errors, which are entirely my responsibility.

CHAPTER 1

The General Nature of Human Language

Afundamental aspect of human language is that it is the primary means for communication among individuals. Oral discourse is the glue that connects members of the society. It is the primary means for the expression of affection and hostility and the principal vehicle for persuasion and social intercourse in human societies. The written language, providing for communication among members of the society not contiguous in space and time, is, of course, parasitic on the oral language and massively extends the communicative function of human language. The manual languages used by individuals who are hearing impaired have all the richness, complexity, and communicative potential of other human languages.

The Creative Nature of Human Language

A remarkable aspect of human language is its creativity. Every day the sentences we hear and produce are completely new. Except for fixed phrases such as "How are you?" and "Have a nice day," our conversations and our reading matter consist of sentences that are different from one another and different from sentences we have heard in the past. Yet we produce and understand sentences of our language with no difficulty and very little conscious effort. The simple and prosaic act of speaking and hearing is really an amazingly creative activity. What is it that we know about our language that allows us to do this? Think of what our sentences have in common despite their uniqueness. Each is made up of words of our language, and each has its words arranged in a pattern that is characteristic of our language. Thus, any collection of words that we know, organized according to a pattern appropriate to our language, will constitute a sentence that we could either produce or understand.

It is at least theoretically possible to list all the words an individual knows (probably around 75,000), although it would be very difficult to actually do so. It is impossible, however, to list all the allowable sentence patterns in a language, simply because there is no limit to how long a sentence can be. For example, "The teacher praised the student who answered the question" is a fine sentence of English, but so is "The teacher praised the student who answered the question that was in the book" and "The teacher praised the student who answered the question that was in the book that was published in England." Rather than try to identify patterns, it is much more reasonable to describe the rules that create the patterns. In the three sentences in the above example, the rule of English for relative clause formation was applied one, two, and three times, respectively.

When words are organized by linguistic rules into a sentence, a structure is created that describes the relationship among the words of the sentence. The meaning of the sentence, then, is determined by the meanings of its words and the structural relationship among them. A great deal is said about the structural organization of sentences later in this book, but a couple of examples will help explain this concept. In English the sentence "John loves Mary" has the simplest structure possible: a subject ("John") and a predicate ("loves Mary"). "Mary loves John" has an entirely different structure ("Mary" being the subject and "loves John" the predicate); therefore, although the two sentences have the same words in them, they have completely different meanings. A slightly more complex example is demonstrated by the following two sentences: "The policeman warned the man who drove recklessly" and "The policeman warned the man and drove recklessly." They differ only by the little words *who* and *and*, but their structures, and therefore their meanings, are entirely different. In the first it is the man who is driving recklessly; in the second it is the policeman.

What we know, then, as speakers of our native language, is a set of words (a *lexicon*) and a set of rules (a *grammar*) to combine those words into sentences with structures indicating the relationships among the words. The rules that create structure, called *syntactic rules*, perform three fundamental kinds of operations. They create sentences with basic sentence structure, which in English is subject–verb–object, such as "John loves Mary." They allow elements of sentences to be moved around; for example, in the sentence "Mary was loved by John" the object of "love," "Mary," has been moved from the end to the front of the sentence. Finally, the syntactic rules allow simple sentences to be combined into complex ones. "The policeman warned the man who drove recklessly" is composed of "The policeman warned the man" and "The man drove recklessly." It is the ability of the syntax to create complex sentences that gives human language its unlimited creativity. The grammar also contains *phonological rules*, which determine the sound patterns of the language, the pronunciation of words, and the prosodic characteristics of sentences. *Morphological rules* govern the way affixes are attached to words to modulate their meaning or allow them to agree with other words. We create sentences by combining the words according to the rules, and we understand the sentences of others by understanding the words and computing the structure of those sentences. It is very useful, then, to be able to distinguish between what we know about a language, its lexicon and grammar, from what we actually do with language, which is speaking and understanding. Traditionally, linguists and psycholinguists refer to the former as *linguistic competence* and the latter as *linguistic performance*.

Linguistic Competence
and Linguistic Performance

Our linguistic competence, then, consists of our knowledge of the lexicon and rules of our language. When we use our competence to produce and understand sentences, we are demonstrating linguistic performance. The subject matter of the discipline of linguistics is linguistic competence; psycholinguists study linguistic performance. The competence–performance distinction is very important in the study of all aspects of human language, especially the study of child language and disordered language. We can only observe linguistic performance, but we often want to know the status of a person's linguistic competence. Many factors other than linguistic competence are involved in linguistic performance (performing on language tests, responding in language experiments, etc.). Thus, to assess people's linguistic competence by observing their linguistic performance (which is the only way to do it), one must be very clever and make sure the techniques provide the best possible answer. This is an issue to which I return repeatedly in this book.

A way to think about the grammar is as a translation device (or a complex code) that allows us to convert ideas into speech (encoding) and recover from the speech of others the ideas that they intend to convey (decoding). Language, however, does not have to be spoken; there are signed languages that have all the grammatical richness of spoken languages. In 1978, Siple reported that American Sign Language (ASL), the language of the deaf in the United States, was the fourth most common language in the United States. It has phonological, morphological, and syntactic rules, but its grammar is very different from that of English (Klima & Bellugi, 1979). The existence of signed languages that are demonstrably full, human languages is of great importance, because it demonstrates that the language capacity of humans is distinct from the ability to speak.

As it is possible to distinguish between language and speech, it is also possible to distinguish between language and thought. One way to demonstrate that thought is independent of language is to note that a single thought can be expressed in any human language; thus, the thought must exist independent of language. A philosopher of language, Jerry Fodor, argued that there exists "a language of thought" in a book by that name (1975). Furthermore, we can think of a variety of creatures who surely can think, but have no language—the higher primates (and probably dogs, cats, and hamsters, as well) and human infants.

Closely related to the distinction between language and thought is the distinction between language ability and general intelligence. Contrary to common belief, these two aspects of development are distinct and can be dissociated. It is part of psycholinguistic lore that the geniuses Albert Einstein and Noam Chomsky did not speak until they were 3 or 4 years old. I cannot attest to the truth of this claim, but children with specific language impairment (SLI) are, by definition, of normal intelligence yet severely delayed in their language development. There are other cases of children with profound intellectual impairments but good linguistic skills. Susan Curtiss (1988) reported on such a young woman, whom she called Marta, who has a testable IQ of 47 but who uses long, grammatically complex sentences. Williams syndrome is a form of mental retardation resulting from a genetically transmitted chromosomal abnormality. Despite their intellectual impairment, children with Williams syndrome acquire language rapidly and have good language skills in every area of language; they have large lexicons, create grammatically complex sentences, and use language socially.

The fact that language is distinguishable from thought and intelligence and the fact that it consists of a set of rules that operate solely on linguistic information have led to what is known as the *modular view* of language and language use. The idea is that human cognition is made up of a number of separate modules that interact with one another. One of these modules is the linguistic system, which operates only on linguistic information, but interacts with other aspects of cognition (memory, real-world knowledge, principles regarding the social uses of language, etc.) to determine actual language use.

We can see, then, that linguistic performance, while underlain by linguistic competence, relies on a number of other nonlinguistic abilities. To decode speech one must be able to hear and perceive the speech correctly and hold a representation of the speech sounds in working memory while computing an analysis of them as a series of words with structure. Thus, a person may fail to understand a sentence that is too long or spoken too quickly or in a noisy environment, even if her linguistic competence is adequate for her to understand the sentence in better circumstances. When we are attempting to test a child's linguistic competence, it is very important to make sure that we are not making the task more difficult because of performance factors unrelated to language. For instance, Goodluck and Tavakolian (1982) showed that sentences such as "The cow bit the pig that jumped over the gate" are easier for 4-year-old children to understand than the structurally identical "The cow bit the pig that kissed the sheep." It appears that having to process a sentence with three animate noun phrases increases the difficulty of a sentence for reasons having nothing to do with the child's linguistic competence.

By the same token, we must be careful not to make our sentences too easy because of factors unrelated to language. Very young children and agrammatic aphasics can understand a sentence such as

"The apple the girl is eating is red" even if they cannot understand "The cat the dog is chasing is black." This is simply because real-world knowledge tells them that girls, not apples, eat things, and apples, not girls, are red; thus, they do not have to decode the first sentence to understand it. In the second sentence, real-world knowledge doesn't help, so to understand the sentence, the child or the aphasic must figure out its structure; in this case they have difficulty. Thus, factors unrelated to linguistic competence can artificially enhance or inhibit a person's performance on tests and experiments.

Similar caveats apply to our evaluation of the language a child produces. It is by no means clear that we can assess a child's grammar solely by observing what she says. The grammar is certainly employed when a person translates an idea into a spoken sentence. After all, the meaning of the sentence is a function of its words and their structural organization. However, other nonlinguistic factors also affect speech production. We know that approximately a clause-sized chunk of an utterance is stored in working memory before speech begins (Garrett, 1988). Speech itself is a highly complex motor skill. Production of a simple sentence requires the organization of over 100 muscles of the mouth, tongue, and respiratory system. A hallmark of the speech of a young child is that sentences are very short, missing "little words" such as *a*, *the*, prepositions, and so forth. A number of studies have demonstrated, however, that children respond to (therefore, mentally represent) words that they do not yet produce. This is a particularly important consideration when one is evaluating the speech of a child with a language problem. Such children typically produce very short, spare sentences. It is crucial to determine whether their production is a result of a deficit in grammatical knowledge or in production ability.

This distinction between linguistic competence and linguistic performance is very important for people whose job it is to evaluate children's language. Communicative interaction always occurs in social contexts, with a great deal of shared information between the child and the people with whom she is talking. Thus, the meanings of the sentences she uses and understands are multiply determined. Children with very slightly impaired linguistic skills are often conversationally quite appropriate, so they are not identified as having a language problem. Later, when they attend school, they may have difficulty learning to read; only then will the underlying language disorder be discovered. The relationship between spoken language abilities and emerging literacy is only beginning to be understood, but it is profound. Many reading difficulties seem to be related to an inability to process linguistic structures. Children with readily observable language impairment in the early years almost inevitably have difficulty with reading when they begin school.

The Uniqueness of Human Language

The creativity described previously is a feature of human language and not of any other naturally occurring animal communication system. Some animal communication systems, such as the dance of the bee (von Frisch, 1953, 1962) and the songs of certain birds (Marler, 1991), are creative in the sense that they consist of units organized into patterns. The dance that the honeybee performs to indicate the location of food and the song a bird constructs to woo his mate do seem to be rule governed in much the same way that human language is. However, these systems lack the creativity of language that derives from the human ability to communicate any thought linguistically. The bee can dance only about the location of food; the bird can sing only to find a mate or mark his territory. Our closest relatives in the animal kingdom, the great apes (chimpanzees and gorillas), have communication systems in the wild that consist simply of a list of calls, each of which has a unique meaning. Their communication systems have no combinatorial power whatsoever.

Many experiments over the years have attempted to teach human-like languages to gorillas and chimpanzees. The most successful of these have been gestural communication systems patterned on, but certainly not as structurally rich as, American Sign Language. Apes can be taught a large vocabulary of individual signs and have even been known to combine a few signs. They certainly engage in communication with their handlers. Through these studies, we have learned a great deal about the cognitive abilities of these remarkable animals, but we have also learned that they cannot be taught a rule-governed communication system like that of humans (Premack, 1976).

The conclusion, then, is that language, if understood to be a system by which words are organized into structures by rules, is unique to humans. It is entirely possible that early hominids such as *Homo erectus* or Neanderthal had linguistic systems similar to ours, but since none of those species still exists, *Homo sapiens* (us) seems to be the only animal with this special kind of linguistic communication system.

Although human languages vary a great deal in their words and grammatical rules (as anyone who has attempted to learn a second language in adulthood can attest), there are a number of basic similarities among the world's languages. Very few words in one language have direct translation equivalents in another (except, perhaps, for purely referential words, such as animal names and body parts). At the same time, lexicons are highly similar in that they all provide the means for talking about the things that humans need to talk about, although fine points of the meaning encompassed by individual words may differ, even in highly related languages. Lexicons are open-ended in that a language may add as many words as it needs as new concepts need to be expressed. For example, many industrialized nations need the word *microchip* in the lexicons of their languages, whereas other cultures can do nicely without it.

We have already alluded to a major similarity among all languages—that is, they all have rules that create structures. Furthermore, all rules of human language are "structure dependent." This means that the rules of syntax always make reference to the structure of sentences rather than to any nonstructural property. We can look to one of the syntactic rules that move things around for an example of a structure-dependent rule. If we want to make a yes–no question out of a sentence such as "The girl is intelligent," we move the verb to the front of the sentence for "Is the girl intelligent?" If, however, the initial sentence is "The girl who is a pianist is intelligent," we do not move the first instance of *is* to the front to form a question. That would give "*Is the girl who a pianist is intelligent?" (The asterisk in front of the sentence means that it is not a well-formed sentence.) Instead, we must move the *is* that is the main verb of the sentence—the verb that agrees with the subject of the sentence—for "Is the girl who is a pianist intelligent?" This is a structure-dependent rule in that the concept of "subject of the sentence" is a structural concept. In our example, the subject of the sentence is "The girl who is a pianist," a noun phrase modified by a relative clause. It could be indefinitely long—"The highly intelligent girl who is a pianist who played at Carnegie Hall . . . . " No matter how complex, the entire structure constitutes the subject of the sentence, and *is* agrees with it. Therefore, *is* is the element that moves to the front of the sentence to form a yes–no question. No human language has a rule such as "move the first verb to the front of the sentence to form a question" or "move the third word of a sentence to the front to form a question" or "say the sentence backward to form a question." Those impossible rules refer to nonstructural properties of sentences. Thus, there are *constraints* on the rules that form sentences, and many of them are the same for all human languages.

Although there are constraints common to all human languages, many features of language structure do vary widely. However, languages seem to be divisible into classes, depending upon the linguistic devices they employ, with sets of linguistic properties clustering together in a relatively small number of classes. One basic division between language types, for instance, is that some languages are right-branching and some are left-branching. This refers to the direction of embedding within complex sentences. In right-branching languages, such as English, relative clauses follow the noun phrase that they modify, whereas in left-branching languages, such as Japanese or Korean, the relative clause precedes. Thus, in English we would say, "The man I saw yesterday was my uncle," whereas in Japanese the sentence would be "Watashi ga kinoo atta hito wa watashi no ojisan desu," literally translated "I yesterday saw the man my uncle is." Whether a language is right- or left-branching is related to its standard word order, with that of right-branching languages usually subject–verb–object and that of left-branching languages subject–object–verb (Goodluck, 1988).

Another example of a basic division among languages is whether they allow sentences without explicit subjects. Languages such as Italian and Spanish, but not English, are so called "pro-drop" languages. They allow sentences such as "Raining" (English would require "It's raining") and "Eats an apple" if the subject of *eats* is obvious from the context (English would require "She eats an apple"). Many aspects of the auxiliary and modal systems are similar for pro-drop languages and differ for languages that do not allow pro-drop (Hyams, 1986).

Linguists have come to refer to these dimensions of variation in human languages as *parameters* (Chomsky, 1981; Hyams, 1986). Some parameters seem to be binary, such as the one that describes whether a language is right- or left-branching. Other variations among languages are not so clear-cut. For instance, languages differ in the degree to which they rely on word order, as opposed to inflections, to encode grammatical information. On one end of the continuum is a language such as English, which has very severe restrictions on word order and no case markings except on pronouns. Thus, information about which is the subject of a sentence and the object of the verb must be encoded by placing the former in initial position and the latter immediately after the verb. Order is the only distinction between the meaning of "The man loves the woman" and "The woman loves the man." On the other hand, German has some constraints on word order, but they are not as severe as those of English because it also has case markings to indicate grammatical relations. Thus, to indicate that the woman loves the man, one may say either "Die Frau liebt den Mann" or "Den Mann liebt die Frau" because the article *den* signals that *Mann* is in the objective case in both sentences. Maximally different from English in this regard is Finnish, which has very few restrictions on word order (other than stylistic preferences) and a rich and complex system of case markings.

I say more about both the universal constraints on grammars and the parametric variation among languages later in this book. These theoretical ideas have played a major role in much contemporary research in language acquisition.

The Biological Basis of Human Language

The fact that language is unique to the human species (species specificity) and similar across languages (species uniformity) leads us to the hypothesis that drives most of modern language acquisition theory: There is a large "innate" component to human language. Innate is in quotation marks because the word means different things in different scientific contexts, so it is important to understand exactly what it means in a theory of language acquisition. Biologists refer to innate birdsong as the song of a bird who has never heard the song of its species. Language acquisition theorists certainly do not mean this, because a child who never heard human language would acquire no language at all. Another use of the term innate in biology is to refer to a characteristic of an individual that develops normally through maturation, needing no environmental input, such as the song of the *Teleoarvllus* cricket (Cairns, 1991; Cairns & McDaniel, 1991; Dawkins, 1986). Goldin-Meadow and her colleagues have for many years studied deaf children of hearing parents who are not exposed to a signed language. Such children develop their own wordlike gestures, known as "home signs," which they combine in order to communicate. The orders that they create are not arbitrary, however; indeed, they seem to invent very rudimentary rules governing word order (Goldin-Meadow & Mylander, 1990). Fascinating as these invented communication systems are, however, we would certainly not want to claim that a full human language would develop without input. Children must experience language, either spoken or gestural, to develop grammar and a lexicon.

What is really meant by the claim that human language is innate is that it is biologically based. Human infants are specially prepared by virtue of being human to acquire a language with the unique features of human language. We know that language is rooted in the neurological system. In the adult, language abilities are lateralized in one of the hemispheres of the cortex of the brain (the left for most right-handed people and 60% to 70% of left-handed people; for others it is lateralized in the right hemisphere). A great deal is now known about how language is stored in the brain, through studies of aphasics, people whose language ability is impaired as a result of damage to the language areas of the brain. Users of signed languages can also develop aphasia as a result of brain damage. They can use their hands for ordinary tasks, but experience difficulty in signing, as aphasics with spoken language have difficulty speaking, although their articulatory organs are unimpaired (Poizner, Klima, & Bellugi, 1987). A variety of other kinds of studies have demonstrated areas of the brain specialized for various functions. For instance, the brain-mapping techniques developed by Ojemann (1983) have demonstrated localization for lexical, semantic, syntactic, and short-term memory functions within the left hemisphere.

We assume that as the neurological system evolved, so did the human's language abilities (Pinker & Bloom, 1990). The similarities among human languages, then, derive from the genetic properties that characterize our species. The constraints on variation in human languages must arise from the fact that only certain forms of representation can be incorporated into the human neural structure.

Despite the very large variation among human cultures, with some seemingly more "primitive" than others, there is no such thing as a primitive language in a human society. People who hunt with bows and arrows and cook on open fires speak languages as complex and sophisticated as those of people in modern industrial countries.

Another argument for the biological basis of language is the phenomenon of the "critical period" for language acquisition. Languages seem to be learned much more easily before puberty than after. Moreover, second languages learned before puberty are usually spoken without an accent, whereas later-learned languages are not (Seliger, Krashen, & Ladefoged, 1975). The unfortunate individual who has not acquired any language before puberty has virtually no chance of ever learning a full human language. Such was the fate of a girl called Genie (Curtiss, 1977; Curtiss, Fromkin, Krashen, Rigler, & Rigler, 1974), who was imprisoned by an abusive father, unable to hear speech, until she was 13 years old. Linguists at the University of California, Los Angeles, attempted to teach her language, with mixed success. She acquired a vocabulary and some rudimentary word order rules, but was never able to acquire the morphological and syntactic rules of English. Newport (1990) studied the critical period effect in users of ASL. All had been using the language for over 30 years, but they differed in the ages at which they had initially acquired it; for some it was their native language, others had learned it in childhood, and still others learned it in adulthood. Newport demonstrated a dramatic difference between those who had acquired ASL in childhood and the older learners. Even the older learners (like Genie) fully mastered word order constraints, but they were markedly inferior to the younger learners in their knowledge of the morphology of ASL. Newport has demonstrated similar effects among people who learned English as a second language in youth versus adulthood. These related phenomena probably all derive from the neurological plasticity of the brain during the critical period. Damage to the left hemisphere of the brain is much less likely to result in permanent aphasia if it occurs before puberty than in adulthood (Foss & Hakes, 1978).

The proposition that human language is innate, then, is really that it is biologically based, in the same way that other characteristically human abilities (e.g., upright posture and the ability to solve problems) are. The neurologist Eric Lenneberg (1967), in arguing for the biological basis of language acquisition, noted that the acquisition of language is more like a purely maturational skill, such as walking, than it is like a skill that must be taught, such as riding a bicycle. It does not need to be taught; all normal children achieve the skill naturally. In fact, the failure to either walk or talk constitutes a pathological condition. Lenneberg also pointed out that each of the biologically determined activities, such as walking and talking, has a regular sequence of development shared by all members of the species.

Uniform development is another kind of species uniformity that creates a very strong argument for the biological basis of the acquisition of language. Everywhere in the world, typical children babble in the first year of life and utter their first word early in the second. Petitto (1992) demonstrated that deaf children who are acquiring ASL also babble gesturally and follow the same developmental sequence in acquiring language that speaking children do. Utterance length is very similar for all child speakers (and signers), and some other properties of early speech are predictable developmentally, even though from the beginning the child's vocalizations reflect properties of the native language, as well. In every human community, language is acquired naturally, without specific instruction. Cultural norms with respect to child-rearing practices vary dramatically among human societies. There are some in which adults speak to children very little, and others in which most parents pay a great deal of attention to communication with their children. Although communication practice varies greatly, language acquisition does not.

Because the word innate has a number of different meanings, it is probably safer to characterize the view that language development is biologically based as *nativist*. The nativist view is that infants are specially prepared neurologically to organize the speech that they hear around them into a grammar that is a possible human language, which is constrained in the ways that all human languages are. Children end up with a richer system of knowledge than would be predicted from the sentences they hear if there were no genetically provided linguistic framework with which to organize those sentences. Although each child learning a particular language hears different sentences in her environment, all children in that linguistic environment end up with virtually identical grammars of the native language. This is because each child is creating the language anew using the same principles of organization. Language acquisition is a special case of the general puzzle identified by the philosopher

Bertrand Russell (1948): "How comes it that human beings, whose contacts with the world are brief and personal and limited, are nevertheless able to know as much as they do know?" (p. 5). Language is by no means the only feature of human cognition that is believed to be biologically based. Developmental psychologists are finding that infants seem to be predisposed to develop such concepts as causality and numerosity without (or with very little) experience (Spelke, 1988).

The experience of children acquiring a creole language is a fascinating and convincing example of the creation of language by children. When people speak different languages and must live and work together, they form what is known as a *pidgin*. This is a combination of the two languages, with common words agreed upon and stitched together with very little grammatical structure. A pidgin does not have the properties of a human language described above. It is a "rudimentary" communication system. When the pidgin speakers have children, however, they hear the pidgin as the language of the environment and create for themselves a language known as a *creole*, which is a fully human language. The organizational powers of the children's biologically based linguistic system have allowed them to form a rich language from an impoverished one (Bickerton, 1984, 1988).

The nativist hypothesis, incorporating as it does the claim that children acquire more language knowledge than would be predicted on the basis of the speech they hear, and also the claim that children do not have to be taught language, has been extremely controversial. It is similar to the nature–nurture debate that has taken place in many areas of human psychology. In the next chapter I explain that the controversial nature of this view of language acquisition derived from the fact that when it originated it was in fundamental opposition to the then-current ideas about language learning. Now all language acquisition theorists believe that there is a nativist component to language acquisition. The differences among them center on two issues: (a) the degree of importance of inborn factors in language development and (b) the question of whether those factors are uniquely linguistic (particular to a language module) or are features of general cognition.

CHAPTER 2

A Theory of Language Acquisition

In this chapter I sketch a contemporary theory of language acquisition, one that assumes that inborn biological factors interact with environmental information as children acquire their native languages. Before moving to current theory, however, it is instructive to take a look at the recent history of the study of language acquisition.

Historical Perspective

The field of language acquisition is one of the areas of psycholinguistics, which, in turn, is a hybrid field that combines the disciplines of cognitive psychology and linguistics. To get a sense of the historical development of language acquisition theory, then, it is essential to examine developments in the fields of psychology and linguistics.

In the late 1950s and early 1960s, psychology adhered to a philosophical position that had begun early in the 20th century. It was conceived of as a science of behavior, as opposed to a science of internal mental processes. The philosophical position was called *behaviorism*, and the psychologists who ascribed to it (virtually all academic psychologists with the exception of psychoanalytically oriented clinicians) were called behaviorists.

The fundamental tenet of behaviorism was that all organisms learned their behaviors according to the same principles of learning, and those principles responded only to the external experience of the organism. No inborn proclivities for particular behaviors were invoked to account for the acquisition of a creature's behavioral repertoire; nor were any internal mental representations assumed to exist. All behavior, then, was to be accounted for by a general *learning theory* that would apply to all organisms, animals as well as humans. Many varieties of learning theories were proposed by psychologists; despite their differences they all had in common the constraint that behavior was to be accounted for solely by describing the experience of the organism under investigation.

Probably the most famous behaviorist of the period was the late B. F. Skinner of Harvard. His learning theory, known as *operant conditioning*, was the most radical of all the theories and was the only one (with the exception of Mowrer, 1954) that was explicitly related to language acquisition (Skinner, 1957). It is conceptually simple and it provides a flavor of the behaviorist perspective. The idea is that an animal will produce a variety of behaviors; those behaviors that are rewarded (reinforced) will increase in frequency and intensity, whereas those that are not rewarded will fade. What appear to be complex behaviors are really only chains of simple behaviors that have been reinforced. There is a famous film of a pigeon Skinner had taught to "bowl." The pigeon would waddle in and hit a Ping-Pong ball with its beak, knocking down a set of pigeon-sized bowling pins. Skinner had *shaped* the bird's behavior by first rewarding him when he walked close to the Ping-Pong ball, then rewarding him selectively only when his beak touched the ball, then rewarding him selectively only when his beak touched the ball hard enough to make it move, and so on, until the individual rewarded behaviors formed a complex chain that gave the appearance of a single motor skill, bowling.

Because the behaviorist philosophy asserted that all animals and humans acquire behavior by the same principles, research was carried out primarily with animals. The principles, however, were extended to humans. The assumption was that speech in humans was a complex chain of individually rewarded behaviors, similar to the pigeon's bowling. The idea was that each infant emits speech sounds, and those of his environment are rewarded by his caretakers. Words are acquired when sequences of speech sounds that combine to make a word are rewarded; phrases and sentences constitute rewarded sequences of words.

This conception of language acquisition fit nicely with the way linguists were thinking about language in the same historical period. They described languages by first describing the sounds of the language, then the rules by which the sounds combined to make words, and finally the patterns by which words formed phrases and sentences. A language was regarded as a complex system of behavior, rather than as a system of knowledge shared by the speakers of the language (a notable exception was Sapir, 1933). There was no conception of the universality of human language or constraints on its form. It was once believed that human languages can vary without limit. This version of linguistics was called *taxonomic* because its primary goal was to discover and categorize the linguistic units of individual languages. In one of the most well-known linguistics books of this period, Bloomfield (1933) explicitly adopted a behaviorist view of language.

This discussion of behaviorist psychology and taxonomic linguistics has been very brief and has left out many details. You can read more about this period in Cairns and Cairns (1976) and Kess (1992). It is also interesting to note that Skinner extended his theories to the realm of language, politics, society, and the question of free will (Skinner, 1973).

The person who changed for all time our conception of language and its use was Noam Chomsky, a young Massachusetts Institute of Technology professor. The papers he wrote in the early 1960s claimed that language is not simply a collection of speech sounds organized into words and phrases; nor is it a complex chain of speech behaviors shaped in the infant; nor can it vary without limit. He said that human language comprises a complex set of rules that are known by speakers of a language and used by them to construct and perceive sentences in that language. Chomsky argued that linguistics should be thought of as theoretical psychology, and that psychology should be considered a theory of mind rather than of behavior. Further, he claimed, there is a fundamental similarity among all human languages, and that similarity is rooted in human biology. Children are not taught language by reward and nonreward, but acquire it naturally through an interaction between inborn structures and experience with the language of the child's environment.

Chomsky's ideas were highly controversial in the 1960s, in both linguistics and psychology. They detonated scientific revolutions in both fields, the repercussions of which are still being played out today. (A man named Thomas Kuhn wrote a fascinating book in 1962 titled *The Structure of Scientific Revolutions*. It is required reading for anyone who wants to truly understand the Chomskian revolution in linguistics and psycholinguistics.) Chomsky remains a controversial figure, but his ideas have changed forever the way we think about human language. Farsighted psychologists such as George Miller (1962, 1965) brought Chomsky's work to the attention of psychologists. Many of them came to understand the importance of his work for the discipline of psychology, and the field of psycholinguistics was born (e.g., Blumenthal, 1967; Brown & Hanlon, 1970; Fodor & Bever, 1965; Mehler, 1963; Savin & Perchonock, 1965).

Contemporary Acquisition Theory

The theory of acquisition that has developed since the early days of the Chomskian revolution is nativist in the sense that it is assumed that those aspects of human language that are universal are part of the biological preparedness that the human infant brings to language. Every human infant has the potential to acquire every human language with equal facility. Each language, in turn, incorporates universal principles of grammar and settings for all the relevant parameters that determine the variation in human languages. The collection of universal principles and parameters of possible variation is known as Universal Grammar (UG). Thus, we say that each child is born "knowing" the universal principles and the potential types of variation his language might incorporate. Each child is born "knowing" UG. This is, of course, a metaphor. What we actually mean is that the child's developing brain will construct only those representations allowed by the constraints on human language. It would be incapable of constructing a rule of grammar such that, for instance, a sentence was made into a question by moving the third word to the front. (Crain & Nakayama, 1986, actually demonstrated that children will not create such a rule.) Such a rule would be impossible in a human language; it would not be structure dependent and could not be constructed within the constraints of UG.

Chomsky is famous for coining the term "language acquisition device" (LAD) to refer to a human child. The child's mind takes as input the speech of the environment, organizes it according to the biologically determined properties of human language, and produces as output the grammar and lexicon of his native language. This enterprise is illustrated in Figure 2.1. The question of how the child receives environmental speech as input to the LAD is itself a major issue. We know that the speech signal is far from transparent in the way it encodes speech sounds. Consider something as simple as the vowel /I/ (as in *little*). It will be physically different depending on whether it is spoken by a man, a woman, or a child (because their vocal tracts are of differing sizes). It also will be physically different if it is in a sequence of fast rather than slow speech. Its physical representation will differ even by the words it occurs in. For instance, it will be different in a word like *kid* than in a word like *tip*. This latter fact is due to a phenomenon called *coarticulation*. When we speak, we do not utter one speech sound at a time. At any single moment our articulators are moving out of one speech sound, into another, and anticipating the next. The result is that the speech signal is continuous, and any single "slice" of the speech signal will contain information about several different speech sounds simultaneously. Thus, the /I/ in *kid* will be pro-

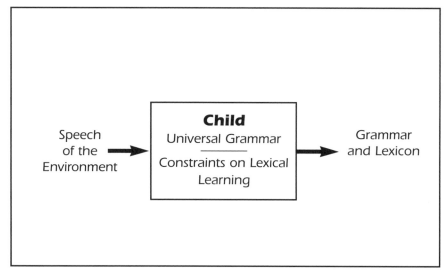

Figure 2.1. Language Acquisition Device

duced as the articulators are moving out of a /k/ and into a /d/, whereas the /I/ in tip is produced between a /t/ and a /p/. Add to this the fact that we do not pause between words; each word runs into the next. So the boundaries between words, as well as the phonemes within them, are hidden within the continuously varying stream of speech.

It is not fully understood how adults, who already know the words of their language, segment the speech stream into individual words. A major question that must be addressed by any theory of language acquisition is how the infant "gets into" the continuous speech stream. Clearly, he must be able to identify some words in the speech he hears and perceive some sort of phrasal organization among them. Psycholinguists think that human infants are predisposed to pay special attention to the prosodic characteristics—the changes of pitch, stress, and duration of fluent speech (Gleitman & Wanner, 1984; Hirsh-Pasek et al., 1987; Morgan, 1986) and that these characteristic prosodic features assist them in their initial entry into the speech stream. A number of researchers have noted that the prosodic characteristics of child-directed (especially infant-directed) speech differ in predictable ways from speech directed to adults. Pitch is higher and intonation is more exaggerated by greater pitch excursions. Fernald (1992) reviewed research from five languages other than English, from a variety of language families, and showed that all contain these features of child-directed speech. She argued that the prosodic characteristics of maternal speech evolved as did other mothering behaviors, such as rocking and stroking, in service of the maternal–infant bond, as well as to provide the infant an entry into the communication system of the species.

An adult understands sentences by creating a representation of words and their structural organization, based on her internalized grammar. The child, however, does not have a complete, mature grammar, so we must ask how he represents the language that he experiences. For this reason, we make a distinction between *input*, the speech that is present in the child's environment, and *intake*, the representations that are actually available to him as information for the creation of grammar at any given period of development. It is not possible, of course, for us to know just what aspects of the speech input are available to the child as intake. Some recent experiments have demonstrated that infants as young as 7 1/2 months old are able to identify words in the continuous speech stream (Jusczyk & Anslin, in press). One of the most exciting areas of research in language acquisition involves the processing of speech by infants. The speech of the environment can be useful only if the child not only hears it, but perceives it, represents it, and uses it as information. This issue is especially important for an understanding of language disorders. One theory of the origin of language disorders is that such children do not process the speech of the environment as successfully as do normally developing children. Although they possess an intact UG, they have a problem in converting linguistic input into intake and using it in the construction of a grammar (Leonard, 1989; Leonard, Bortolini, Caselli, McGregor, & Sabbadini, 1992).

Figure 2.1 shows that the child constructs a grammar, but obviously he does not construct a complete adult grammar instantaneously. It would be more accurate to show that he constructs a series of grammars, ending with the complete grammar of his language. (This process may not be complete for some children until very late childhood.) We want to be able to describe the intermediate grammars that the child constructs on his way to having a complete grammar of the language. Each of the intermediate grammars is immature (or incomplete) from the point of view of the mature grammar, but each is the grammar of a possible human language. Put differently, the child's intermediate grammars must conform to Universal Grammar. Helen Goodluck (1988, 1991) has called this the "no wild grammars" constraint on child language. The theory that all intermediate grammars conform to Universal Grammar is known as Continuity Theory (Pinker, 1984).

An example of a feature of child language that conforms to UG, but not to the language of the environment, is the phenomenon of subjectless sentences in child English. It is a well-attested phenomenon that English-speaking children use subjects optionally, producing sentences such as "Change pants" and "Papa change pants" (Braine, 1973, cited by Hyams, 1986). Sentences without subjects are ungrammatical in adult English, but they do not violate UG. Many languages, such as Spanish, Italian, and Chinese, allow sentences without subjects if the speaker and hearer both understand who the subject is. So it is possible to say "mangia una mela" ("eats an apple") in Italian if everyone knows who is eating the apple (Hyams, 1986). Thus, we can see that this intermediate grammar, one allowing subjectless sentences, while it is not English, does not constitute a violation of Universal Grammar.

The Child's Linguistic Input

A goal of a complete theory of language acquisition is to be able to describe exactly what information the child must extract from the speech of the environment to enable him to construct a grammar (and a lexicon) of his language and how that information must be presented to the child. Let us first think of the kind of information the child needs. It is not enough for him simply to hear grammatical sentences; he must experience sentence–meaning pairs (Crain, 1991). Hearing "The dog is chasing the cat" is useless unless one is able to pair that sentence with the nonlinguistic event of a dog chasing a cat. The sentence provides information about the correct word order of English only if there is some nonlinguistic way for the child to know that the sentence describes an event in which the dog is the actor and the cat is the object of the action. The process of relating basic sentence structures and simple events in the world (via a process known as *linking rules*) constitutes what Pinker (1984) has called *semantic bootstrapping*. In this way, the child "gets into" simple sentence structures by relating them to observed events in the world.

If the child needs to experience sentence–meaning pairs, it is pretty clear that speech presented without paired actions, such as one hears over the radio, would not suffice for language learning. What about television? Would passive exposure to speech on television constitute an adequate format for the child to acquire a grammar? Obviously, it would be unethical to perform experiments of this nature, but Sachs, Bard, and Johnson (1981) had the opportunity to observe a naturalistic test of this question. They reported the case study of two hearing children of deaf parents, who were discovered by a team of speech pathologists. While (unlike Genie, discussed in Chapter 1) the children had been reared in an affectionate home environment that met their physical and emotional needs, they only experienced language by watching television; their parents did not sign with them. The older child, Glen, was 3 years old when Sachs and her colleagues began to study the children. He knew some words and could combine them, but the organization of the words was aberrant.

Some examples are "That enough two wing," "Off my mittens," "This not take off plane." None of these sentences is typical of a child his age. His younger brother, Jim, who was 18 months old, did not speak at all. The speech pathologists visited Glen at regular intervals and had conversations with him. They did not attempt to teach him language, but they provided a communicative linguistic environment for him. In 6 months his language was age appropriate, and he became the language model for his brother. From this and similar anecdotal reports, we can guess that it is highly likely that, for language acquisition to be successful, the child's linguistic input must be in the form of social, interactive speech. An interesting exception to this observation comes from statements by their children whose parents speak a second language. Such children often appear to acquire the second language passively, much to the chagrin of their parents, who believe they cannot be understood. This "passive" learning is of a second language, however; it should not constitute a counterexample to the hypothesis that first languages must be acquired interactively.

Beyond the reasonable supposition that the child's input needs to be in the form of interactive, communicative speech, it is of great theoretical interest to know exactly what are the necessary properties of the child's linguistic environment and the language to which he is exposed for acquisition to take place. In recent research this question has been addressed by attempting to assess the role of the caretaker in the acquisition process (apart from producing speech with special prosodic properties). Within this body of research, there are two discernible threads. The first is concerned with the extent to which the child requires feedback from the environment, and the second deals with whether the speech the child hears must have special characteristics.

We no longer take seriously the view that children must be rewarded for structurally correct utterances and nonrewarded for incorrect ones. An early study by Brown and Hanlon (1970), conducted during the early days of psycholinguistics when the Chomskians were battling with the behaviorists, actually investigated this question. They showed that parents reward truthful statements whether or not they are structurally correct according to the adult grammar. For instance, a child in their study (Adam) was approved for the sentence "Draw a boot paper," but disapproved for "And Walt Disney comes on Tuesday," because it was inaccurate. In a more recent work (titled

"Brown and Hanlon Revisited"), Hirsh-Pasek, Treiman, and Schneiderman (1984) reported a similar concern with accuracy as opposed to structure.

Clearly, then, parents do not regularly point out to their children the errors that they make. In fact, children seem quite resistant to explicit correction. A famous example is the following exchange between a child and parent (reported by McNeill, 1966):

CHILD: Nobody don't like me.

MOTHER: No, say "nobody likes me."

CHILD: Nobody don't like me.

(Eight repetitions of this exchange)

MOTHER: No, now listen carefully; say "nobody likes me."

CHILD: Oh! Nobody don't likes me.

It has been suggested, however, that more subtle sorts of corrections and expansions from the caretaker may play a role in language learning. An important study by Cazden (1965), replicated by Feldman (1971), showed that expansions are less effective in accelerating language development than are relevant conversational replies. The distinction between these two types of response is illustrated by the following: If the child says "Doggie running," an expansion response would be "The doggie is running," whereas a relevant conversational response would be "Yes, and isn't he cute?" Newport and Gleitman (1977) reported some instances in which expansions affect performance on certain aspects of structure, such as use of the auxiliary. They (see also Gleitman, Newport, & Gleitman, 1984) suggested that expansions are useful only when they provide grammatical information for the child at a moment when his attention is focused on the particular form–meaning pair. They are not useful for signaling to the child when he has produced an ungrammatical sentence.

Thus, there is an important kind of information that is *not* available to the child in his environment. This is information about what structures are not part of his language. Psycholinguists call this *negative evidence*; no one tells him he is wrong, corrects him consistently (or successfully), or in any way gives him sufficient information about ungrammatical forms to assist significantly in language learning. There may be some parents who are very conscious of their child's grammatical "errors" (some such people may be reading this book) and really do spend a lot of time correcting the child's language. Such parents usually think they are doing the right thing and are providing a good linguistic environment for their child. The best advice for such parents is that they should relax, merely make sure they communicate effectively with their children, and not drive the poor kids nuts about their language. (Kids need to enjoy talking.) While such parents certainly exist, parental input of this type could not possibly operate as a causal factor in language acquisition theory. For this to be the case, every parent everywhere would have to do it and every child everywhere would have to follow his parents' advice. This is obviously false. Finally, even if every ungrammatical utterance every child in the world produced were corrected by caretakers, we still could not rely on negative evidence to account for language acquisition, because children must acquire rules that mark as ungrammatical sentences they have never had the opportunity to say. Everyone reading this book knows that "Himself was shaved by John" is an ill-formed sentence of English, but we could not have acquired that knowledge by each of us saying a sentence of that form to our parents and being corrected for it. Many parents naturally assume that they play a major role in "teaching" their children language (while they would not for a moment think they had taught the child to walk), but a moment's reflection demonstrates that this could not possibly be a major factor in a general theory of language acquisition. We assume, then, that the child has access only to information from the environment about what is possible in his language, not what is impossible. We characterize this by saying that the child must build his grammar (and, it also turns out, most of his vocabulary) based solely on *positive evidence*. This fact has profound consequences for an understanding of how the child acquires knowledge of his language. We must account for every grammatical development that we observe by showing how it could have been acquired without negative evidence.

To see how we can account for development without appeal to negative evidence, let us look at a real example from the acquisition of English. It has been demonstrated that children go through a period (under the age of 3 or 4) when they think that a reflexive pronoun can function like a personal pronoun. Thus, they will think that "Grover patted himself" can mean that Grover patted Ernie, as well as that

Grover patted Grover. How can they ever learn that *himself* can refer only to the subject of such a sentence? No one tells them (this would be negative evidence). Sure, they only hear *himself* being used reflexively, but that is positive evidence. If they think *himself* can also be used to refer to someone outside the sentence, they will think that they just haven't happened to hear anyone use it that way yet. Maybe next week. After all, there are many grammatical constructions that a child (or an adult, for that matter) hasn't heard yet. Language would be impossible to learn if the child assumed that everything he hadn't heard was ungrammatical.

We know that children eventually acquire the grammatical knowledge that "Grover patted himself" can only mean that Grover patted Grover and not that Grover patted Ernie. We know this because we know that adults have this grammatical knowledge (and children grow up to be adults). We also know it because studies have demonstrated that children have this knowledge by the age of about 4 (McDaniel, Cairns, & Hsu 1990). How do they acquire this knowledge in the absence of negative evidence? There is a general principle of language that reflexives of a certain type must always refer to the subject of their clause. This is part of Universal Grammar. Once the child has classified *himself* as a reflexive of that type (and as distinct from personal pronouns), he will be able to apply the universal principle of language. Thus, the child's access to UG allows him to acquire a grammatical principle without negative evidence. This account relies, however, on the acquisition of lexical information, in this case that *himself* is a reflexive rather than a personal pronoun. There is, however, a lot we don't know about lexical learning. I have a great deal more to say about this particular example and other similar universal principles in Chapter 4. It is always a challenge, in developing a theory about how children move from one grammar to a more advanced one, to formulate the account with the assumption that they have only positive evidence available to them. These problems are called problems of *learnability*. It is not enough simply to formulate descriptions of the child's grammar at various points in time; we must also account for the learnability of each succeeding grammar.

We know, then, that a critical function of the speech of the environment is to provide children with positive evidence regarding the structures produced by the grammar of the language they are attempting to acquire. Psycholinguists have asked whether there are special properties of caretaker speech to children that are necessary to provide a linguistic model for them. It has been shown that adults as well as older children speak differently to infants and younger children than they do to each other (Shatz & Gelman, 1973). The speech adults address to infants and children is semantically simpler than the speech they address to other adults and is, as one would expect, geared to the cognitive level of the child. Structurally, it is also less complex. Sentences are shorter, with fewer embedded clauses, simpler verb phrases, and so on (Hoff-Ginsburg & Shatz, 1982; Snow, 1977). This type of speech has been nicknamed *motherese*.

What we need to know is whether this type of input is necessary to the language acquisition process or whether it has any relationship to the speed of language acquisition. There must clearly be some properties of the language input that are essential for language acquisition. It must be processable by the child, both structurally and semantically. If a child heard only discourse about international affairs in sentences with structures far beyond his processing ability, he would probably have some difficulty acquiring language. On the other hand, if he heard only speech of the form he produces, he would never receive sufficient information to make progress. In fact, a clever study by Shipley, Smith, and Gleitman (1969) demonstrated that children respond best to speech just a bit above their current level of production. Furthermore, they probably need to hear a great variety of structures in their language, so oversimplified input is not an advantage. Gleitman et al. (1984) have indeed demonstrated that, to the extent that fine variations in caretaker input can be shown to have an effect on subsequent child language, children seem to progress more rapidly with a richer input.

This issue—the speech of the developing child's environment—goes far beyond simply describing general features of caretaker speech, or motherese. What we need to understand for a complete theory of language development is exactly what sort of input from the environment the child must receive to develop a grammar of his language. Thus, with respect to studies of caretaker speech, we would like to know if there are particular features of that input that are related to particular features of the child's developing language. Obviously, such studies are very difficult because caretakers provide a great variety of forms and children are rapidly acquiring many features of language.

The best attested relationship between caretaker speech and a particular feature of child language was identified by Gleitman et al. (1984). They found a statistically reliable relationship between the mothers' yes–no questions and the children's acquisition (or, in any event, use) of the auxiliary system. How can we explain Gleitman et al.'s finding that the more yes–no questions mothers used, the earlier auxiliaries appeared in the speech of the children? A very important aspect of the child's grammatical development depends on the acquisition of the auxiliary system of the language. These are words like *is* in "The cat is jumping" or *has* in "The cat has jumped." (I say more about the development of the auxiliary system in the next chapter.) These are precisely the units of sentences that are moved to the front in yes–no questions because they agree with the subject of the sentence (e.g. "Is the cat jumping?" "Has the cat jumped?"). Perhaps by using many yes–no questions, the mother provides the child with positive evidence about the auxiliary system of English. In yes–no questions, the auxiliary element is distinguished from the rest of the predicate, and it is made perceptually salient because it appears in sentence-initial position. Notice, however, that the incidence of yes–no questions in maternal speech accelerated only slightly the acquisition of the auxiliary system. If we did not have a construction that moves the auxiliary into a perceptually salient location, children would still learn the auxiliary system of English, using other kinds of information.

Developmental psycholinguists want to identify what information in the child's environment is necessary and sufficient for language acquisition to take place. We want to do this purely to further our theoretical understanding of normal language development and desire no practical application of that knowledge. It is unnecessary to improve on nature; a normal linguistic environment will provide normally developing children with the information they need. For people dealing with children with language disorders, however, knowledge about input speech is highly practical. If a child is not developing language normally, the entire therapeutic enterprise is about providing input to facilitate language development. Theoretical and empirical discoveries about necessary information for language development are absolutely crucial for the development of intervention strategies in speech–language pathology. It is unlikely that we will make such discoveries by naturalistic studies of caretaker–child language. We need good intervention studies of normally developing children that investigate the effects of theoretically motivated features of language on specific features of language development.

What is meant by "theoretically motivated features of language"? The linguistic theory that we are using can give us ideas about the kinds of information children need to develop grammars. Two examples can be drawn from facts about English discussed earlier in this chapter. We said that for a child to acquire a grammar requiring coreference between *Grover* and *himself* in the sentence "Grover patted himself," *himself* must be classified as a reflexive pronoun. When this happens, a universal principle of language will become engaged in the child's grammar. Thus, we know that this is the kind of lexical information the child needs for this aspect of development. Because all normally developing children acquire this feature of their grammar before the age of 4, we assume that this information is readily available in the child's environment.

Another example comes from our discussion of parameters of language variation. In English, all sentences must have subjects, even if they are not needed for the meaning of the sentence. Thus, an English speaker must say "It's raining," whereas an Italian speaker can say the Italian equivalent of "raining." Early child language (English as well as other languages) contains many subjectless sentences. The English-speaking child needs to obtain information from the environment to allow him to set this parameter of his grammar correctly. Put differently, he needs information that will allow him to figure out that subjects are not optional, but are essential in the language he is acquiring. Remember, this can be achieved only through positive evidence. Children are not corrected for leaving out subjects, and it wouldn't change things if they were. The mere fact that children hear sentences with subjects isn't enough; languages such as Italian, which allow subjectless sentences, also allow sentences with subjects. Anyway, children acquiring English also hear sentences such as "Want lunch now?" in casual conversation. What the English-acquiring child must have in his input are sentences with *meaningless* subjects such as "It's raining" and "There is a book on the table." Of course, children hear such sentences from infancy, so why do they use subjectless sentences until they are 2 1/2 or 3 years old? This highlights the distinction between input and intake. Perhaps the child has to be at a certain point in language development before he can pay attention to the presence of meaningless subjects in the speech of the environment. It may be a question of the child's being able to process ambient speech thoroughly enough to identify subtle features such as the one that distinguishes the meaningless (expletive) subject *there* from the "pointing" (or deictic) *there*. It may even be that the child has to hear a great many sentences with meaningless subjects before he is confident that he should alter his grammar to conform with a different parameter setting. This example highlights how acquisition theory can reveal important features of environmental language, as well as many of the salient questions that remain unanswered.

There is currently some debate about exactly how children set the parameters of their language. According to one view, each parameter is initially set to its unmarked setting (e.g., to allow subjectless sentences), and a particular feature of the language of the environment (e.g., the presence of meaningless subjects in our example) is said to *trigger* the switch to a grammar set for the other value of the parameter (Hyams, 1986). According to another view, Universal Grammar provides the child with a set of hypotheses about how his language might work. His task, then, is to listen for evidence in the speech of the environment that will allow him to determine which of the possible human variations his language represents (Valian, 1990). We need a great deal more information about how children acquire the correct parameter settings before this debate can be settled. However, the latter view, which depicts the child as a more active language learner than the former, seems more likely to comport with what we know about the nature of early child grammars and about the linguistic input that determines those grammars.

Another subject of debate in acquisition theory is the role of maturation in language development. Obviously, there are some effects of maturation, such as the fact that the first word appears around the same age for children everywhere (Slobin, 1973) and the fact that during the first 2 years of life there is an explosion of neural connectors in the left hemisphere of the child's cortex (Foss & Hakes, 1978). We have already suggested, as well, that the shortness of children's early utterances is a result of the limitation, due to immaturity, of their working memory system. The issue under debate, however, is whether children acquire aspects of UG by maturation or whether the entire grammatical framework is available to them as soon as they have the lexical knowledge and processing abilities to use it. I make this question more concrete in Chapter 4 when I address details of grammatical development.

Biological Preparedness for Language

In the last 20 years, a great deal of research has confirmed the hypothesis that human infants are biologically prepared to acquire language and indicated that human infants are born with physiological and perceptual abilities specialized for speech. Condron and Sander (1974) showed that prelingual infants synchronize their gross bodily movements with the prosody and structure of human speech. Called *interactional synchrony*, this behavior is exhibited in response to many varieties of human speech other than the child's native language, but not in response to nonspeech sounds. (Adults demonstrate interactional synchrony with conversational partners.)

The left hemisphere of newborns is typically larger than the right, and they are able to distinguish between human speech and other nonspeech sounds. Furthermore, this perceptual distinction is enhanced when stimuli are presented to the left hemisphere (Entus, 1975; Molfese, 1973). Very young infants show a preference for listening to speech rather than to nonspeech; they also show a preference for their mother's voice and prefer their native language to a nonnative one (Mehler et al., 1990). In the womb babies can hear only the general prosodic contours of speech, since the sound waves are damped by amniotic fluid. Languages and the speech of individuals do differ prosodically, so some of the learning that leads to these preferences may take place before birth. In any event, these results demonstrate that infants are sensitive to linguistic distinctions when they have had only minimal experience with language.

It is well known that if we can see someone speaking, the speech is easier to understand than if we can only hear the speaker. This has been experimentally demonstrated by degrading speech so that it is difficult to understand (Sumby & Pollack, 1954). Perception is far better if the speaker is in view. This shows that we have internalized knowledge about the relationship between speech sounds and the articulatory gestures used to produce them. This is not surprising, however, because, after all, we know a language that allows us to produce speech sounds. It appears, however, that infants who have not yet produced speech also have a sense of the relationship between articulatory gestures and speech sounds. Spelke and Cortelyou (1981) presented infants 10 to 16 weeks of age with tape-recorded speech and films of two women, one speaking the words that were being heard and the other speaking something different. The infants preferred to look at the film in which the woman was speaking the words on the tape. McKain, Studdert–Kennedy, Spieker, and Stern (1983) replicated these findings and demonstrated that the preference is more pronounced when the visual presentation is processed by the left hemisphere.

Until now I have managed to avoid technical language, but to facilitate understanding of the next few experiments described, I need to introduce the concept of the *phoneme*. Every language employs a variety of speech sounds; some of them are used to distinguish words from each other and some are not. For instance, in English /p/ and /b/ are used to distinguish words; we have *pig* and *big*. There are two types of /p/s, one like the /p/ in *pig* and the other like the /p/ in *spin*. The former is aspirated, and the latter is not. (Put your hand in front of your mouth and you will feel a puff of air when you say *pig* but not when you say *spin*.) The speech sounds that keep words distinct from one another are called phonemes; so /p/ and /b/ are different phonemes of English, but aspirated and unaspirated /p/ are not. There are languages, however, in which aspirated and unaspirated /p/ are phonemes. Each language selects from all the possible human speech sounds a small set that are distinctive. It is a linguistic universal that all languages have phonemes; which phonemes they are is specific to individual languages, however. The phonemes of a language exert a special influence on the perceptual systems of adults. Speech sounds that are members of the same phoneme will sound similar to one another even if they vary phonetically, and speech sounds that are members of different phonemes will sound completely different even if they are phonetically very close. This is known as the categorical nature of speech perception; it is more pronounced for consonants than for vowels. Thus, the adult's perceptual system seems specially tuned to detect best those sound differences that are distinctive in his language.

In a well-known series of experiments, Eimas and his colleagues (cited in Eimas, 1975) demonstrated that prelingual infants divide a speech continuum perceptually in much the way adults perceive distinctions between, but not within, phonemic categories. Because the babies in these studies do not yet possess a linguistic system in which the existence of phonemes could create perceptual categories, their categorical perception of speech constitutes an inborn perceptual ability necessary to the acquisition of a phonemic system. There is abundant evidence that the infant speech perception system develops rapidly. Kuhl (1992) demonstrated that infants could recognize vowels and syllables as similar when they were spoken by male, female, and child talkers. She also showed that 6-month-old infants perceive certain vowels as better exemplars of their vowel category than others; these are the vowels that are more phonetically "pure" versions of their vowel category.

Werker and her colleagues (e.g., Werker & Lalonde, 1988) made the remarkable discovery that 6-month-old infants perceive differences between speech sounds that are not phonemic in the language they are learning as sharply as do adult speakers for whom the distinction is phonemic. For example, Hindi makes a phonemic distinction between /t/ produced with the tongue tip touching the back of the teeth and /t/ produced with the tongue tip touching the ridge at the front of the roof of the mouth (called the alveolar ridge). English does not make such a phonemic distinction. These two types of /t/s are perceptually highly distinct for Hindi speakers, but to English speakers they sound the same. In one of Werker's many studies, 6-month-old infants perceived the difference between the two kinds of /t/ as well as do adult Hindi speakers; 10-month-old infants perceived the difference less well than did the 6-month-olds; and 1-year-old babies performed like English-speaking adults, having lost the ability to distinguish the two kinds of /t/. The ability to perceive distinctions between speech sounds that are phonemes in the child's language is, of course, maintained at adultlike levels.

It appears, then, that in the realm of speech perception we have an example of exactly the scenario our theory suggests. The infant is born with the ability to distinguish perceptually all the human speech sounds that are potential phonemes. Through experience with the speech of the environment, he identifies the phonemes of his language and incorporates them into his grammar. It is highly interesting that the perceptual distinctions between nonphonemes disappear about the time the child is beginning to acquire a vocabulary, which is filled with words that are kept distinct by phonemes. We know that children are particularly adept at acquiring other languages throughout childhood, so it is certainly not the case that the perceptual categories are immutable. If a child is fortunate enough to acquire more than one language, he has no trouble developing the phonemic system of the new language and a perceptual system to deal with it. Adults, however, are known to have difficulty perceiving phonemic differences when they attempt to learn a second language. It is certainly not impossible, but more difficult for the adult than for the child.

If it is true that language is part of our genetic endowment, acquired over centuries of evolution, as were other species-specific characteristics, then we would expect that many inborn disorders of language would have a genetic basis and, therefore, would be heritable. It is beginning to seem as though this is the case, at least for some varieties of language disorders (Tallal, Ross, & Curtiss, 1989; Tomblin, 1989). Gopnik (1990) has conducted what is known as a "pedigree" study of many generations of a family with a history of language disorders. She has traced the inherited links throughout the family tree. Sometimes the manifestation is specific language impairment (SLI), which Gopnik calls developmental dysphasia; sometimes learning disabilities; and sometimes dysfluency. Her work seems to confirm what speech–language pathologists have suspected by observation, that language disorders do run in families.

The fact that language disorders are heritable does not, however, tell us what is being inherited. It could be that Universal Grammar is impaired in children with specific language impairment. Or it could be that UG is intact but that children with SLI are unable to process the linguistic input from the environment in such a way as to develop a fully human grammar. Or it could be that the children do develop linguistic competence normally, but have difficulty deploying it in the comprehension and, particularly, in the production of sentences. Serious research in language disorders, informed by acquisition theory, is in its infancy, so it is too early to answer any of these questions. It is definitely the case, however, that research in normal language acquisition will be key to developing a theory of abnormal development. By the same token, the study of abnormal language development will be of critical importance in our understanding of normal development.

CHAPTER 3

The Course of Language Development

In this chapter I describe the course of language development in the English-speaking child. This description provides a framework for a closer look at the acquisition of morphology and syntax in the next chapter and conversational skills in Chapter 6. This developmental sequence is an idealization, however. Many perfectly normal children do not go through all these developmental periods. Although the overall course of language development is similar for all children, there are great individual differences in the details. Some babies babble productively; others rarely babble at all. Some children produce their first word before their first birthday; others, not until 18 months or even older. In general, girls talk earlier than do boys and have a lower incidence of speech and language problems. First-born children usually talk earlier than those in other birth orders. These are all tendencies, however, that do not hold for all children.

Language disorders often present themselves initially as language delay. In fact, while speech–language pathologists have long debated the distinction between language deviance and language delay (Leonard, 1972), it is true that the primary symptom of a language disorder may be severe language delay. However, only about 5% of 5-year-olds have specific language impairment (Tomblin, 1993). Thus, if a child seems to be delayed in language development, it is important to try to figure out whether it is an acceptable delay that will likely correct itself or a delay that is a precursor to a long-term language problem. A language delay always presents itself as a delay in production. In evaluating the delay, however, it is necessary to consider the child's receptive abilities and even general nonlinguistic communicative skills. Some recent research (Thal & Tobias, 1992) suggests that children who are late talkers but good general communicators tend to catch up, whereas children who are generally communicatively delayed are more likely to have a real language problem.

The developmental course described in this chapter refers primarily to the child's production of speech and language. Receptive skills are dealt with in more detail in subsequent chapters. The developmental sequence described here is not restricted to children acquiring spoken language. Petitto (1992) demonstrated similar patterns of acquisition for children acquiring American Sign Language. The existence of similar developmental sequences for spoken and signed languages is strong confirmation of the view that language is represented as a separate module of the mind, independent of the modality in which it is instantiated.

The First Year of Life

In the prelingual infant we see evidence not only of biological preparedness, but also of precursors to a wide variety of linguistic properties of later speech (Lieberman, 1980; Stark, 1980). In the second half of the first year, the soft coos of the very young infant give way to syllabic babbling which, though it has no content, seems to be constructed of nonsense "words" with phonetic segments and the prosody of simple sentences (Oller, 1980). The phonetic elements at this point are typically open vowels and simple stops in sequence, with a great deal of duplication. Although these babbled utterances sound like words, they are not true words, because they do not have consistent referents. Similarly, strings of the babbled nonsense words sound like sentences, with rising and falling intonation. Of course, they are not true sentences because they have no structure or meaning. Some characteristics of the prosody of the language the child is to acquire is present in the babbling of this period. Furthermore, the babbled consonants and vowels bear phonetic resemblance to those of the infant's target language (Boysson–Bardies, Sagart, & Durand, 1984).

Although the early stop consonants of this period sound a great deal like those of the adult, acoustic studies show that they are indeed quite different because the infant lacks the vocal and laryngeal control to produce the synchrony between closure and voicing required for the adult production of these sounds (Allen & Hawkins, 1980; Kewley-Port & Preston, 1974).

The first year of the infant's life is a period of great change in the articulators and the control mechanisms necessary for speech. At birth the larynx is high and close to the oral cavity, and the tongue is proportionally much larger than it is for the adult, so the vocal tract is very small. During the first year, the larynx moves down and the cortical control mechanisms necessary for articulatory synchronization and timing develop rapidly. As mentioned earlier, from birth until the age of 2 there is an explosion of neural pathways in the area of the left hemisphere of the brain, which is responsible for the motor control of speech. Motor neurons undergo myelination, the development of protein sheaths that insulate the nerve and prevent impulses moving along one tract from short-circuiting others. The development of myelin sheaths is essential for all highly synchronized motor activity. The confluence of these factors allows the infant to begin to produce sound sequences that are clearly language-like and are precursors of sentences (Foss & Hakes, 1978).

As the infant is developing physically, she is developing socially as well, and many properties of the adult–child interaction are precursors of the social interaction and pragmatic functions of later language. The turn-taking of conversational discourse is presaged by the locked gaze and interactive cooing and babbling exhibited by young infants. Nonverbal gesturings exhibit some of the earliest functions of language, such as requesting, and some of the most primitive meanings, such as negation.

In describing the stages of cognitive development, Piaget (1952) labeled the first 2 years of life the period of sensorimotor intelligence. During this period the infant discriminates herself from the rest of the environment and elements in her world from one another. She begins to form internal representations of the world; Piaget believed that these representations are stored in the same manner in which they are experienced, in patterns of motor activity and direct representations of sensory experience (Flavell, 1963; Piaget, 1952). Recent work suggests, however, that some of the child's representations of the world are more abstract and may exist prior to direct, interactive experience (Spelke, 1988). The fundamental knowledge that the child acquires during this period concerns the location of objects, her power to act on them, and their effects on one another. By the end of the first year, infants have developed the knowledge that objects exist even when hidden. It is now known that the precursors of this ability can be demonstrated in infants as young as 3 1/2 months old (Baillargeon, 1987). This is known as *object permanence* and is assumed to be a cognitive prerequisite for naming (Bloom & Lahey, 1978), since to know a word for something requires that one have a mental representation not only of the word, but also of the named object.

By the end of the first year, then, everything comes together for the child; the development of object permanence and the articulatory control to form wordlike sound sequences. The result is the child's first word, signaling the beginning of a period during which virtually all of her utterances will be one word in length.

The One-Word Stage

The first word usually occurs when the child is about 1 year old in all the cultures we know about. Beyond this period, there is some correlation between age and linguistic sophistication, but there is also a great deal of individual variation. It is, therefore, difficult to set specific ages associated with linguistic milestones. It is, however, possible to be secure in a description of the sequence of development and the general characteristics of the speech of children in a fairly large age range. The first words typically refer to things and events in the "here and now" and tend to be words referring to things that move, act on other things, and are acted upon by the child. Thus, words such as *bottle, shoes,* and *car* are in most children's early repertoires, which rarely include words for immobile nonmanipulable objects such as *couch* and *floor*. The largest proportion of early words are nominals, followed by action words (those that elicit or accompany action), with these two categories comprising the vast majority of the early lexicon for most children (Benedict, 1979; Nelson, 1973).

It has long been noted that the child's first words are not merely referential, and that the same word can mean different things in different contexts. "Milk" uttered while pointing at a glass of milk in the distance can mean "I want some milk," but can mean "I spilled the milk" in the context of a puddle of milk beneath the high chair. The one-word period has been referred to as the *holophrastic* stage to express the notion that each single word refers to a whole phrase whose meaning must be inferred from context. Of course, there is little evidence that the child actually has linguistic knowledge of sentences or phrases, but it is clear that these single words carry a conceptual burden beyond referential naming. Dore (1974) suggested that these early words express primitive speech acts and as such are the precursors of more sophisticated speech acts that will be part of later pragmatic development. In a complementary and not necessarily contradictory analysis, Greenfield and Smith (1976) characterized these early words as expressing relationships that the child conceptualizes in a nonlinguistic form. These relationships are closely tied to the child's cognitive development and reemerge in the two-word stage.

As speech begins, the infant develops the phonemic system of her language gradually. The initial phonemes are those that are the simplest in an articulatory sense and are present in the majority of the world's languages. These are the pure stop consonants and vowels that are produced with an open vocal tract. In the stops, distinctions between place of articulation (e.g., /b/, which is made with closure of the lips, vs. /d/, which is made with closure behind the teeth) will be acquired before voicing contrasts (e.g., /b/, which is voiced, vs. /p/, which is not). Continuants, such as /f/ and /s/, come in later, and the last speech sounds to be pronounced correctly are the liquids (/r/ and /l/) and the complex affricates (/ʧ/ and /ʤ/). These generalizations greatly oversimplify the findings of a great deal of research (see, e.g., Ingram, Christensen, Veach, & Webster, 1980; Macken, 1980). The volume in this series that deals with language disorders of children (Schwartz, in press) contains an excellent review of the acquisition of the articulatory and phonological systems.

A great deal of variation occurs among children acquiring different languages, among children acquiring the same language, and even within individual children with respect to the acquisition of individual speech sounds. Needless to say, because children have a phonemic inventory that is smaller than that of the adult language and because they cannot produce articulatory gestures of great complexity, early words are characterized by simplification processes of various kinds. Quite common, for example, is the substitution of less complex sounds for more complex ones (Cairns, Cairns, & Williams, 1974). Thus, stops are frequently substituted for fricatives and glides (/w/ or /y/) for liquids. Other simplification processes that do not seem to involve the substitution of a less for a more complex speech sound are voicing and assimilation processes described by Ingram (1988). Consonants tend to be voiced when they precede vowels and devoiced at the end of syllables (e.g., /dos/ for *toes* and /bɛt/ for *bed*). Assimilation means that the consonants in a single word will be produced with similar points of articulation. Thus, *duck* may be pronounced /gʌk/, with the consonants assimilating to the velar point of articulation, or *tub* pronounced /bʌb/, demonstrating labial assimilation. Unstressed syllables are often deleted as in the familiar "nana" for *banana*, and consonant clusters are simplified well into early childhood. Some general principles of cluster reduction are observed in most children. In general the least complex of a phoneme cluster is retained and the more complex sounds reduced. Thus, children often say /kul/ for *school*, /pay/ for *play*, and so on.

Most likely, the normally developing child's misarticulations do not arise from a misperception of the words in the language of the environment. The child appears to believe that her pronunciations are more nearly correct than they actually are. Anecdotal accounts similar to the following abound: I corrected a child of my acquaintance when he pronounced *spaghetti* "pusgetti" (an error virtually universal to English-speaking children), and he replied indignantly, "I didn't say pusgetti—I said pusgetti." The child probably is not actually misperceiving either the adult or herself, but simply lacks the motor skill to match her production to her perception. Some errors in speech production, however, are a result of the fact that the underlying phonological system of the child is not as fully developed as that of the adult. The phonological rule system is part of the child's developing linguistic competence, whereas articulation (speech) is an aspect of linguistic performance. Thus, the child's early speech evinces the interaction of developing competence and developing performance. (For an excellent treatment of these issues, see Schwartz, in press.)

The child's intonation of the early words is similar to that of short sentences, with terminal contours of rising or falling pitch at the end. As the child's vocabulary builds, related words are uttered in sequence, but they still have the prosodic shape of two one-word utterances. When the two juxtaposed words form a unit, the intonational contour joins them, with the intonational fall (or rise) occurring only after the second word, and the child has entered the two-word stage of acquisition (Bloom & Lahey, 1978, p. 148).

The Two-Word Stage

As George Miller was explaining Chomsky's ideas to the field of psychology in the 1960s, Roger Brown of Harvard University, motivated by the relevance of those ideas for language development, was conducting the first psycholinguistic studies of child language. He and his graduate students studied the language of three children, whom they called Adam, Eve, and Sarah (Brown, 1973). A great deal of what is now known about early language production was first learned by Brown and his students in those studies and has been borne out by further research. They recorded naturalistic speech from the three children and analyzed it in an attempt to describe the children's developing linguistic systems. Adam, Eve, and Sarah's speech samples are now stored in the CHILDES system, which stands for the Child Language Data Exchange System and contains many databases of children's productive language (MacWhinney, 1991; MacWhinney & Snow, 1985, 1990). Other important early work describing early speech was done by Menyuk (1969) and Bloom (1970).

What we are calling the two-word stage is the same as Brown's Stage 1, which is the first of a sequence of stages he identified based on the mean length of utterance (MLU) of the three children he studied. MLU is counted in terms of morphemes, rather than words. A morpheme is commonly defined as the smallest meaningful linguistic unit. A word can constitute a *free* morpheme, which stands alone. Other morphemes must be *bound* to a word; for instance, the past tense marker is a bound morpheme. Thus, the word *purred* consists of two morphemes, the word *purr* and the past tense morpheme, in this case expressed orthographically by the letters *ed* and phonetically by the phoneme /d/. English is not a highly inflected language, which means it does not have as many bound morphemes attached to its words as some other languages (e.g., Italian or Spanish) do. Furthermore, a characteristic of early English is that many of the bound morphemes are omitted. Thus, MLU turns out, in the early stages, to refer to the average length of the child's utterances in words. Stage 1 was defined as extending from the first multiword utterance to an MLU of 2. Eve was 18 months old when she achieved an MLU of 2, whereas Adam and Sarah were 27 and 29 months, respectively.

A great deal of research has been done on the structure and meanings of the two-word utterances characteristic of Stage 1 speech. (See Bloom & Lahey, 1978, and Brown, 1973, for excellent reviews of this literature.) The basic finding is that children of this developmental level use their utterances to express a relatively small set of semantic relations. Declarative utterances encode the following relations (Brown, 1973, p. 173):

RELATION	EXAMPLE
Agent and action	Mommy push
Action and object	Pull car
Agent and object	Mommy cookie
Action and location	Walk street
Entity and location	Baby table
Possessor and possession	Mommy sock
Entity and attribute	Big doggie
Demonstrative and entity	That doggie

In addition to declarative sentences, the child utters negative sentences of three types. In order of increasing complexity, these are nonexistence ("all gone milk"), rejection ("no dirty soap"), and denial ("No truck," referring to a toy car) (Bloom & Lahey, 1978). Two types of questions are observed: yes–no questions uttered in English with rising intonation ("Doggie there?") and wh– questions (limited to "what," "where," and occasionally "who"), also with rising intonation.

These semantic relationships are the same as those expressed in the one-word stage characterized by Greenfield and Smith (1976). Children are commenting on actions, locations, and states of objects in their immediate world. Cross-linguistic studies indicate that the content of Stage 1 speech is very similar for all the languages studied. Furthermore, children of this age use their utterances for the same functions in languages across the world: to name objects, make demands, describe events and objects, indicate possession, negate, and question (Slobin, 1973). These facts point to the universality (and biological basis) of the cognitive development of children of similar ages learning different languages around the world (Slobin, 1985). They also point to the modularity of language as a system separate from general cognition.

While early speech is similar in meaning for children acquiring different languages, the structures (as well as the lexical items) with which these semantic relations are expressed differ dramatically (Slobin, 1973). The influence of the environmental language is obvious in these earliest utterances, as children do not combine word pairs randomly. The English restriction on word order, which is the result of a parameter to be discussed in the next chapter, is rigidly observed by English-speaking children. Thus, agents precede verbs, verbs precede objects, adjectives precede nouns, and so on. English is not a highly inflected language; it does not require lexical items to be marked indicating case, nor is there a rich system of inflections affecting gender and number agreement among words in a sentence. Early utterances in English, therefore, display little grammatical complexity beyond word order constraints. This fact led some early researchers to suggest that young children have very little capacity for grammatical organization in their linguistic systems. Studies of children of comparable age and linguistic sophistication learning highly inflected languages, however, show that the language of very young children can be grammatically quite complex (Slobin, 1985). For example, Italian is a language that requires agreement between determiners and the nouns they precede in both gender and number. Hyams (1986) reported that children younger than 2 years have mastered this system, producing utterances such as "questo mio bimbo" ("This is my [male] baby") in which all three words are inflected for the masculine singular.

The two-word stage is as interesting when we consider what children do not say as when we consider what they do say. There are two classes of words, *content words* (also known as *open class*) and *function words* (also known as *closed class*). Content words are *verbs, nouns, adjectives*, and *adverbs*, which have independent meaning. Function words, on the other hand, are words that, while not without meaning, serve primarily grammatical functions. These are words such as conjunctions, articles, prepositions, and the like. During the two-word stage, the overwhelming majority of a child's words are content words, with very few function words. Neither do we find the copula or any system of modals (e.g., *would, could, might*) or auxiliaries. Although an occasional pronoun such as *you* or *me* might be used, there is no system of pronouns, reflexives, and reciprocals (e.g., *each other*). A system of quantifiers (e.g., *each, every*) is also missing, although individual quantifiers such as *some* may appear. In terms of content, these children do refer to events and objects displaced in space and time, but they do not use counterfactuals, hypothetical statements, or subjunctives. In terms of language use, they demand, but they do not persuade or drop hints. The subtleties of language come later.

As the child moves from the two-word stage, utterances lengthen and develop rapidly in formal and semantic complexity. The length of the stage varies from child to child. Roger Brown's Eve was in Stage 1 for only 1 month, whereas Adam and Sarah each spent 3 months in Stage 1.

Unusually short sentences are characteristic of the speech of children with language disorders. For instance, Leonard (1994), in comparing the mean sentence length (in words) of children developing language normally versus those with language disorders, reported that whereas a normally developing child might achieve a mean sentence length of 3.1 at 30 months, 4.1 at 37 months, and 4.5 at 40 months, the child with a language disorder would achieve these mean sentence lengths at 63 months, 73 months, and 79 months, respectively. Furthermore, even when sentence length increases, children with language disorders continue to have difficulty mastering the auxiliary system. For a list of predicted mean sentence lengths from 18 to 60 months, see Miller (1981).

Language Beyond the Two-Word Stage

Sentences longer than two words at first involve no increase in structural and semantic complexity. Length increases by what Brown (1973) called the "law of cumulative complexity," so that utterances represent combinations of the basic structural and semantic units present in the two-word stage of development. Brown described a number of processes:

1. *Conjoining.* In this process, overlapping expressions, such as action–verb and verb–object, are combined. Thus, the child who has previously said "Boy hit" and "Hit ball" now says "Boy hit ball."

2. *Expansion.* In this process, elements of simple grammatical relations are replaced by noun phrases expressing other grammatical relations. Thus, in an agent–action expression, the agent may be represented by a possessive noun phrase, yielding, for example, "My cookie all gone," or, for an action–location, "Sit Adam chair."

3. *Elaboration.* The basic declarative sentence incorporates the elements agent, action, object, and location. As utterances expand beyond two words, three and more of these expressions are included, but they always appear in the order prescribed by English. Examples are the following: "Adam ride horsie" (agent–action–object); "Tractor go floor" (agent–action–location); "Adam put truck window" (agent–action–object–location).

As utterances initially expand beyond two words in length, they encode the same grammatical relations as did the initial two–word utterances, the only difference being that more grammatical relations are encoded in a single utterance. Brown's notion of cumulative complexity also applies to the combination of these basic, Stage 1 semantic relations into the first longer sentences.

As the child's sentences lengthen, they have a number of identifiable properties. Function words and many inflections are absent, to be added gradually in a somewhat predictable manner. These early utterances have been described as "telegraphic" because they are missing only those little words that adults edit out of their telegrams. "See doggie play bone" illustrates the common characteristics of omission of subject, articles, and prepositions, as well as the lack of a tense marker on the verb or the inclusion of a modal or an auxiliary in the verb phrase. The omission of bound morphemes is a central feature of the speech of children with specific language impairment. These children use them for the first time later than do children who are acquiring language normally, and it is much longer until they use them consistently. In fact, some never use all bound morphemes in linguistic environments in which they are obligatory for the language (Leonard, Bortolini, Caselli, McGregor, & Sabbadini, 1992).

Another characteristic of this period is that sentences rarely contain elements that have been moved. *Wh–* questions are produced without inversion, so the child says "Where that doggie is?" rather than "Where is that doggie?" Yes–no questions are also produced with rising intonation ("Doggie there?") rather than with the inverted "Is the doggie there?" I have much more to say about question formation in the next chapter.

Just as children resist moving elements in their early syntactic constructions, they also resist inserting an element into their sentences. Thus, their early use of the negative tends to be at the ends of sentences, as in "Me fall no" or "Not baby medicine." Only later do children place the negative element inside the sentence; about this time, they are beginning to use negative contractions, such as *don't* and *can't* for sentences such as "Baby don't fall."

In Brown's study of Adam, Eve, and Sarah, he determined that there was a regular order of acquisition of 14 morphemes, some bound and some free. This order of emergence seems to be similar for most children acquiring English (Brown, 1973). Brown's 14 morphemes and their order of acquisition are as follows:

1. *Present progressive.* This is the bound morpheme *ing* in a sentence such as "The kitty is sleeping." Children do not use the auxiliary *is* until much later. A typical sentence would be "Kitty sleeping."

2. & 3. *The prepositions* in *and* on. These, of course, are free rather than bound morphemes.

4. *Plural.* This refers to the orthographic *s* that is bound to nouns, as in *dogs.* Brown does not include in his list the acquisition of the irregular plural, such as *children* or *mice.*

5. *Past irregular.* Irregular past tense forms, such as *broke,* appear before regular past tense forms.

6. *Possessive.* This is also an orthographic *s,* as in "Grover's."

7. *Uncontractible copula.* The copula is the verb *to be.* It can be contracted in sentences such as "He is there," becoming

"He's there," but not in environments such as "Here I am." "*Here I'm" is not grammatical. It is in the latter environments that children first use the copula.

8. *Articles.* These are the free morphemes *a, an,* and *the.*

9. *Past regular.* Regular past tenses are orthographically *ed,* as in *worked.*

10. *Third person singular (regular).* This again is an orthographic *s,* as in "He works." Note that the plural third person "They work" is the uninflected form of the verb, as used in infinitives such as "They like to work," without a bound morpheme.

11. *Third person singular (irregular).* This affects words such as *does* and *has.* Again, the plural is the infinitival form (*have* and *do*), with the exception of the verb *to be,* which becomes "They are."

12. *Uncontractible auxiliary.* The auxiliary can be contracted in some cases; for example, "They are cheering" can become "They're cheering." But in "They were cheering" the auxiliary *were* cannot be contracted. Like the copula, the uncontractable form appears first in children's speech.

13. *Contractible copula.* See the example in number 7.

14. *Contractible auxiliary.* See the example in number 12.

Basically similar but slightly different orderings were found by de Villiers and de Villiers (1973). For a comparison of their ordering with that of Brown (1973), see Nelson (1993).

An interesting phenomenon is associated with the regular plural and past tense morphemes. Children tend to overgeneralize them to irregular cases, so that they say things such as "sheeps" and "tooths" (sometimes "teeths" and "childrens") and "eated" and "goed." In fact, children who begin using irregular past forms, such as "ate" and "went," switch when they acquire the rule to form the regular past tense. It is as though they have removed the irregular forms from their lexicon when they discover that there is a regular rule for plural and past tense formation. It sometimes takes years for all the irregular forms to return, and the children still often overgeneralize the irregular past in place of the particular form, producing phrases such as "I had went" (which is grammatical in some dialects of English, whereas the use of "goed" for the past tense is not).

Overgeneralization is a very interesting feature of language acquisition. It is absolutely universal; all children do it. It means that they produce forms that they have never heard, in a rule-governed way. Thus, it is an excellent example to demonstrate that children do not learn language by imitation, but by the internal construction of the rules of their language. The question of how a child recovers from her overgeneralizations is a learnability puzzle. We assume that she receives only positive evidence; every child is not corrected every time she says "drinked" (this would be negative evidence). So how does she ever learn that there aren't two forms of each of these verbs, *drank* and *drinked*, but she hears the latter form only from her child friends? One proposal is that there is a constraint in Universal Grammar that a language cannot have two forms that mean the same thing. This is Pinker's (1991) *uniqueness principle*, which is discussed in Chapter 5.

Along with the auxiliary system comes the use of modals, such as *can* as in "I can go," when the child's MLU is about 3.5 (Klima & Bellugi, 1973). Acquisition of the modal *do* opens the door to other common kinds of errors. When *do* is introduced, it is supposed to carry tense, but children frequently put the tense marker redundantly on both the *do* form and the verb (Valian, Winzemer, & Erreich, 1981), producing sentences such as "I didn't spilled it" rather than "I didn't spill it." Before the development of the full modal system, we observe the use of such words as *can't* and *don't*. Thus, a child produces sentences such as "He not little" and "She can't stand up," but not more advanced sentences such as "You can sit down," with the modal *can* (Klima & Bellugi, 1973). At this period *don't* and *can't* are called *fixed forms*, another commonplace in child language. A fixed form is a word that is constructed in the adult language (*can't* is the contraction of *can* and *not*) but learned as a single lexical item by the child. Only later when the entire modal system is in place does the child construct such words as an adult would. Fixed forms can also refer to entire sentences. A child of my acquaintance once enjoyed exclaiming "I can't believe I ate the whole thing" (a sentence from a television commercial) although complex sentences were not yet present in his speech.

A fundamental feature of all human languages is that they have devices for combining simple sentences to make complex ones. The ability to do this enables us to encode complex ideas and construct indefinitely long sentences. The first precursors of this ability in early speech are the use of the fixed forms *gonna, hafta,* and *wanna.* Whereas for the adult these are contractions of *going to, have to,* and *want to,* they seem to function initially as single words for children. These forms also participate in the first multiple-verb sentences most children produce, such as "I wanna go potty" (Bloom, Lahey, Hood, Lifter, & Fiess, 1980). These are followed by precursors of the infinitive, such as "I want Mommy get it," and later the adult form, "I want this doll to stay here" (Bloom, Tackeff, & Lahey, 1984). Other complex sentences are those using coordination, with the first conjunction being *and*: "He was stuck and I got him out." Conjunctions with subordinating clauses are later: "It must be mine if it's a little one" (Limber, 1973). Other early constructions are object complements, such as "Watch me draw circles" and "I see you sit down." The construction of these sentences appears to obey Brown's (1973) law of cumulative complexity, as they simply contain in object position a sentence the child has typically constructed in isolation. *Wh–* complements are also early forms, such as "I don't know who it is," as are headless relatives such as "Look-a what my made" (J. J. Stafford, personal communication). Both of these structures are characterized by Hamburger and Crain (1982) as precursors of relative clauses. These are later occurring forms, such as "I want the one what you got" (*what* is frequently used as a relative pronoun) and "I want something that the cows eat."

The production of complex sentences begins around the age of 3 or a little earlier, when the MLU is close to 4.0. These early complex sentences have a number of interesting properties. They have very simple structure, with few of the complementizers used by adults, such as "I know *that* he is here," "I want her *to* come," or "I like eat*ing* pizza." The embedded clause is always at the right end of the sentence, as is all increased complexity in the early utterances of children speaking right-branching languages. The first complex noun phrases are at the ends of sentences; we are more likely to hear "That a blue flower" than "Blue flower right there." Early coordinated noun phrases tend to be in object position rather than subject position (Bloom et al., 1980); thus, we hear "Mommy's gonna get me chair and table" more often than utterances such as "Uncle Paul and Grandma not there." In early complex constructions, clauses never occur in subject position, as in "That you came early surprised me." The relative clauses follow the same pattern, always modifying the object (as illustrated above) rather than subject noun phrases. Menyuk (1969) reported a few subject-attached relatives among kindergarten children, but not a significant number until first grade. Very useful descriptions of the development of complex sentences can be found in Menyuk (1969, 1978) and Nelson (1993).

We have learned a great deal over the past three decades about language acquisition through the study of children's speech. However, we must not lose sight of the fact that a child's productive language, while underlain by grammatical knowledge, is determined by a number of other factors. Thus, it may not accurately reflect the child's grammar (competence). In many cases it appears that children know more than they say. In the next chapter I explore many of the ways psycholinguists have attempted to obtain information about children's linguistic competence.

CHAPTER 4

Acquisition of Syntax

The nativist theory of language acquisition that is adopted in this book is succinctly represented in the description of the Language Acquisition Device (LAD), diagrammed in Figure 2.1. Central to this theory is the proposition that there are universal aspects of human language that are biologically instantiated in the human infant. It has been the task of theoretical linguists to describe those language universals, and the task of developmental psycholinguists to gather data to further our understanding of the acquisition process. Thus, for the past 30 years there has been an interaction between linguistic theory and acquisition data that is paradigmatic of the relationship between theory and data in all sciences. Experiments are designed and conducted within a theoretical framework that essentially identifies what features of child language are the most interesting to look at. The data that result from those studies then reveal something new about the developmental process and often suggest alteration of the theoretical framework. Thus, the relationship between theory and data is dynamic and mutually dependent. As was pointed out in the preface, good empirical research, while informed by theory, advances knowledge independently of any particular narrow theoretical formulation. Research in developmental psycholinguistics illustrates this process beautifully. Over the past 30 years remarkable progress has been made in understanding language acquisition through an interaction of changing theoretical formulations of the internal structure of the LAD and strong empirical research.

I made the point in Chapter 1 that the meaning of a sentence is determined by the interaction of the meanings of its words with their structural organization. Syntax refers to that aspect of a language that creates and describes the structures available for the construction of meaningful sentences in that language. Some properties of the syntax of every language are universal principles, and some are particular to that language. Furthermore, many of the language-particular characteristics seem to be parameterized; that is, large groups of languages share that particular feature or parameter setting. The theoretical framework used in this book to describe English is thus called the Principles and Parameters approach. Perhaps the most important point of all is that there are many structures that no human language can have. This is because there are universal constraints on the rules that create syntactic structures in human languages. These constraints are captured in the Principles and Parameters framework. The nativist theory of language acquisition assumes that the child is biologically prepared to respond to the speech of his environment by creating an internalized grammar that will obey the universal principles, select among the available parameters, and obey the universal constraints on syntactic structures.

This is not a book about the Principles and Parameters approach in linguistic theory. In the preface I mentioned some good introductory sources for those readers who would like to read more about the theory. Some technical terminology is essential, but I try to keep it to a minimum. The goal of this chapter is to describe what is known about the development of many aspects of the English-speaking child's grammar, as well as to highlight some important unanswered questions.

The Structures Available to the Child

One of the functions of syntax is to create and describe the basic sentence structures of a language. Thus, an important goal of linguistics is to create a vocabulary and a notational system that can convey all the information necessary for the description of basic sentence structure. That structure is created by linguistic rules and is displayed in diagrams known as phrase markers. The most basic structure of an English sentence was once described as in Figure 4.1, a noun phrase (NP) subject and an auxiliary (Aux) system (which contains information about the tense of the verb, and person and number features of the subject, with which the verb must agree), followed by a verb phrase (VP) made up of a verb, and an object noun phrase (which is optional). It was often necessary to also have as part of the sentence structure a complementizer, so structures like that in Figure 4.2 were also used. The uppermost sentence node was known as an "S-bar"

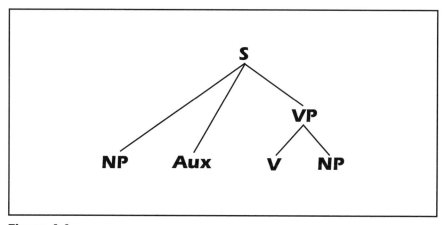

Figure 4.1

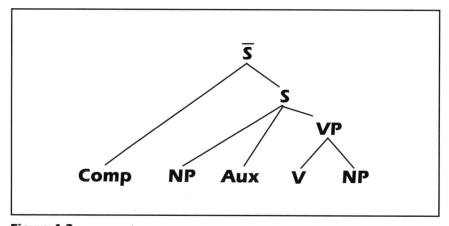

Figure 4.2

(sort of a super S), which dominated a *complementizer* (Comp) and a sentence (S). Complementizers are words such as *that* in the sentence "He knew that Grover was hungry." The Comp position was also useful as a "landing site" for moved elements, such as the auxiliary *is* in the question "Is the bear sleeping?"

A more contemporary description of the full structure made available by the grammar for an English sentence is given in Figure 4.3. It is basically a hierarchically organized network of *phrasal nodes*. The diagram looks very different from the basic sentence structures in Figures 4.1 and 4.2, but it is actually not very different. The uppermost phrase is a *complementizer phrase* (CP), which does much of the work of the S-bar structure in Figure 4.2. IP stands for *inflectional phrase* and is analogous to the S of Figures 4.1 and 4.2. The reason a sentence is now called an IP is because an inflectional system (the old auxiliary) is basic to every sentence. Each phrase is composed of a *specifier*, a *head*, and a *complement*. I illustrate this with the phrases in Figure 4.3. First

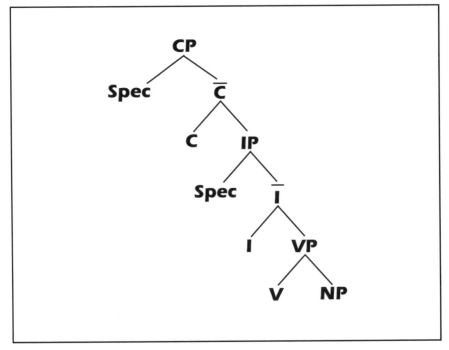

Figure 4.3

comes CP; I have indicated its specifier (Spec) and will explain momentarily how it is used. The C with a line over it is called C-bar and is often written as C'. It is only an intermediate node that dominates the head of the phrase and its complement. In the case of CP, the head is C, which stands for *complementizer*, and its complement is IP. The specifier of IP is the subject of the sentence, and its head, I, which stands for *inflection*, carries information about the tense of the sentence and the number and person of the subject. The complement of IP is VP, which stands for *verb phrase*. Its head is V, for verb, and its complement is NP, *noun phrase*, which is the object of the sentence, if it has one. The NP also comprises a specifier, an intermediate node, a head (the noun), and a complement; however, we don't need that much structure for the purposes of this chapter. In fact, some linguists break IP down further into a tense phrase and an agreement phrase (for person and number), but we do not need an analysis of nearly that detail.

To describe a sentence with only a subject, verb, and object, such as "The girl petted the cat," we would have a structure as in Figure 4.4, with *the girl* in the specifier of IP; *pet* in V; the past tense, third person, and singular features in I; and *the cat* as the object NP. We would not need the complementizer or the specifier of CP. In fact, we often use structures as in Figure 4.1 or Figure 4.2 as "shorthand" if we do not need all the structure provided by the grammar. Thus, the structure of "The girl petted the cat" could be represented either as in Figure 4.4 or in the more sketchy Figure 4.5. The structure in Figure 4.5 is an acceptable shorthand representation if we need to convey no more information about the structure than it makes available.

In a yes–no question such as "Is the girl petting the cat?" *is* (with features expressing tense and agreement with the subject) would move from I to the complementizer position (C), and everything else would be the same. In a yes–no question such as "Did the girl pet the cat?" the modal *did* would carry the tense and agreement features. Finally, we would use the specifier of CP to describe a *wh–* question such as "Whom did the girl pet?" *Whom* would be in the specifier of CP, *did* would be in C, *the girl* would be in the specifier of IP, and *pet* would be in V. But what happened to the object of *pet*? Indeed, *pet* needs an object, so the NP should not be empty; furthermore, we know that the question word *whom* is asking precisely that question—what is the object of *pet*? The way the structure captures this is illustrated in Figure 4.6. We assume that there was an underlying structure

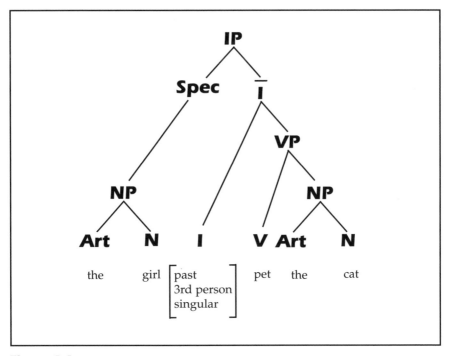

Figure 4.4

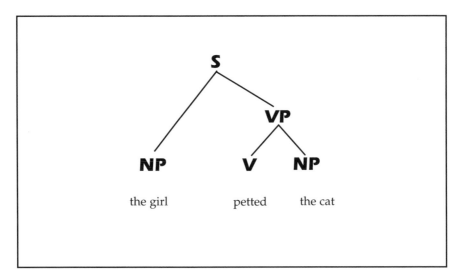

Figure 4.5

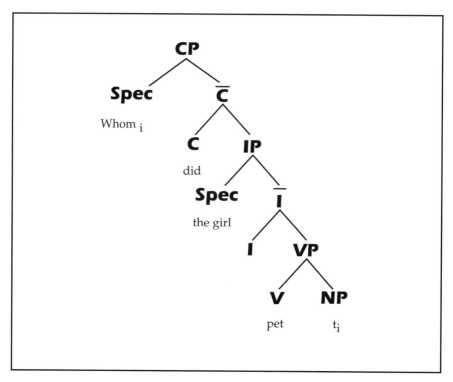

Figure 4.6

(known as a *deep structure* or *D-Structure*) that had a question word in the NP. According to the rules of English, it moved to the front of the sentence, but left behind a *trace* (represented by a lowercase *t*). To indicate that the *wh–* word and the trace refer to the same entity, they have the same *index*, in this case *i*. Anytime we have a structure that contains two words that must refer to the same thing, we capture that fact by giving them the same index in the structural representation of the sentence.

The phrasal nodes whose heads are words, such as noun and verb, that are represented in the lexicon, are called *lexical phrases* or *lexical categories*. There are phrases for all the various types of words—adjective phrase, adverbial phrase, prepositional phrase, and so on. The phrases that have nonlexical heads (e.g., inflection and complementizer) are referred to as *functional categories* or *functional phrases*. These are CP and IP in our diagram.

Functional Categories, Auxiliaries, and Bound Morphemes

Some of the features of early child language have been explained by some acquisitionists as indicating that the child's early grammar lacks functional categories, incorporating only lexical ones. Radford (1990) proposed that early structures are only VPs. According to his analysis, the Stage 1 child's sentences lack inflection, auxiliaries, and modals because IP is not yet represented in the child's grammar. Auxiliaries and modals carry the features represented in I. Thus, if there is no I, there would be no inflections on verbs and no grammatical role for auxiliaries and modals. According to Radford, there are no movement operations in the Stage I child's grammar because there is no CP to provide sites to which *wh*– words can move. Thus, the subject of early child sentences is represented in the specifier position of VP. These early sentences consist of a subject, an uninflected verb, and (optionally) its complement.

It has also been suggested that the grammars of children with specific language impairment (SLI) lack functional categories. This accounts for the fact that they so often omit the bound morphemes that are tense and agreement markers. Wexler (1994) argued against this analysis for both children who are normal and those who are language impaired (Rice & Wexler, in press), suggesting instead that all children go through a stage in which tense marking is optional, so verbs are not always inflected for tense, even though IP is present in the child's structures. He called this the "optional infinitive stage" and presented data from a variety of languages to support his analysis.

Leonard (1992, 1995) also argued that children with language impairments do, indeed, have functional categories in their grammars. That is, they have access to all the structure described in Figure 4.3. In a careful analysis of a number of children with SLI, he showed that they have all the morphosyntactic features of the normally developing child, but they appear later in development and are not used as consistently as they are by normal children. Neither normally developing nor SLI children confuse bound morphemes; they simply omit them. Leonard suggested that the acquisition of bound morphology, for both tense and agreement marking, is a two-step process. First, the child must analyze the speech of the environment and represent the morphology correctly in his grammar. Second, over time the morphological elements increase in strength in the grammar. Both of these processes are involved in the acquisition of bound morphology for both normal and SLI children, but deficits at both stages delay SLI children, first in their initial identification, then in the achievement of consistent use.

Smith-Lock's (1993) two-stage theory, which she calls the "Linguistic Analysis Hypothesis," is very similar to Leonard's. The first stage is identical to Leonard's: The child must analyze the language of the environment and perceptually identify the morphosyntactic elements to incorporate into his grammar. The second stage is slightly different from Leonard's. Smith-Lock suggested that the child must monitor and analyze his own speech and make sure that the morphemes are used whenever they are required. This is compatible with Menyuk's (1991) suggestion that language delays in children are caused primarily by their inability to bring to awareness what they know about language. According to all three of these related accounts, the SLI child has a fully specified Universal Grammar available to him, but his ability to analyze both the speech of the environment and his own is impaired. Thus, he is later in representing the morphology in his grammar and unable to use the morphemes reliably in speech. In a major series of experiments comparing children with SLI from the age of 5 years, 4 months, to 7 years, 3 months, to age-matched and language-matched control groups, Smith-Lock gathered data supporting her hypothesis. Tasks included production of bound morphemes and judgment and correction of morpheme errors. The children with SLI performed identically to the language-matched groups (who were 3 years, 3 months, to 4 years, 3 months), but significantly worse than the age-matched groups. Of particular importance was the judgment and correction task. Presumably, the children's ability to carry out that metalinguistic task (see Chapter 6 for a definition and discussion of metalinguistic skill) reflected their ability (or inability) to carry out the kind of self-analysis and self-correction required to use bound morphemes reliably in speech.

Gopnik (1990) presented a very different analysis of the origin of bound morpheme errors in the speech of children with SLI. She suggested that the child with SLI suffers from "feature blindness" and is unable to represent in his grammar the syntactic features of tense, number, plurality, and so forth. This would be an impairment of Universal Grammar. She argued that the fact that such children do not use the morphological markers consistently suggests that they do not have a systematic representation of the features encoded by those markers. This analysis was presented in her study of an 8-year-old English–French bilingual child. Among his errors were plural markers ("You make one points"); use of articles preceding proper names and gender errors ("The Red Riding Hood arrive at his grandma's house"); third person singular markers ("One machine clean all the two area"); and two kinds of errors on progressive constructions ("The dragon jumping" and "The dragon is walk"). Gopnik pointed out (as did Leonard, 1995) that the hierarchical syntax of such children is far less problematic than their use of bound morphemes.

A serious problem in work with children with SLI is that they form a very heterogeneous group. There may be multiple reasons for language impairments in the entire population of SLI children. A great deal of valuable information is being obtained by psycholinguists and language pathologists who are trying to develop theories of impairment that are informed by theories of normal language acquisition.

Subjectless Sentences

As mentioned earlier, children acquiring English and a great many other languages often omit subjects, although subjectless sentences are not grammatical in the language they are learning. There is a dramatic subject–object asymmetry; objects are not omitted with nearly the frequency that subjects are. The phenomenon of subjectless sentences has also been explained by the suggestion that early child structures lack functional categories. According to Radford's (1990) analysis, subjects in the specifier of VP are not required to be present. Subjects are required in English only if they occupy the specifier position of IP. In fact, many people have noted (the first was Hyams, 1986) that when English-speaking children acquire auxiliaries and modals their subjectless sentences disappear. The same phenomenon has been noted in SLI children. They produce subjectless sentences until a much later age than do normal children, but the same relationship exists between the emergence of auxiliaries and modals and the abandonment of subjectless sentences.

Hyams (1986) was the first to give a parametric account of subjectless sentences. She noted that in many languages of the world sentences without spoken subjects are fully grammatical, whereas in others (e.g., English) sentences must have subjects even if they are meaningless, as in "It's raining." These two types of languages represent two different "settings" of the "sentence subject" parameter. Hyams hypothesized that all children initially have grammars that reflect the setting of that parameter that allows subjectless sentences. Children acquiring Italian or Spanish never need to change their parameter setting, as it is correct for their languages. English-speaking children, however, must receive positive evidence so that they will reset their parameter, requiring that all sentences have overt subjects. Sentences with meaningless subjects could constitute the positive evidence English-speaking children need to change their parameter. Hyams further noted that subjectless sentences disappear when children develop auxiliaries and modals in their speech; thus, she hypothesized that IP is restructured when the English-speaking child's grammar changes to require overt subjects.

A more current analysis than Hyams's early one relates the subjectless sentence period to Wexler's (1990) optional infinitive stage (Hyams, 1994). Valian (1990, 1991) and Bloom (1990) suggested that early sentences lack subjects for reasons related to the child's processing limitations; thus, they claimed that the subjectless sentence phase is a performance rather than a competence phenomenon. It is far beyond the scope of this book to explore all the analyses of early subjectless sentences; there is now a huge literature on this topic. What does seem fairly certain is that a strong connection exists between this phenomenon, the development of IP (including the features incorporated in I), and the acquisition of modals and auxiliaries. Furthermore, this is a salient feature of speech of children with SLI and yet another example of a normal process that seems to be delayed in children with language impairments. Connell (1986) developed an intervention technique designed to teach children with language disorders to use subjects consistently.

Word Order

The basic word order of English is captured by the fact that the heads of all the phrases precede their complements. The fact that the specifier of IP and its head, I, precede its complement, VP, and that the head of VP precedes its complement, NP, is what accounts for the fact that the word order of the basic English sentence is subject–verb–object. Whether a language has heads first or last in its phrases is a basic parameter of human languages. Left-branching languages have heads last; right-branching languages have heads first. It has long been noted (Slobin, 1973, 1985) that very early child speech (as early as the two-word stage) honors the word order restrictions of the language the child is acquiring. Poeppel and Wexler (1993) and others have observed that the head order parameter is one that is set very early for all children. Fernald (1992) wanted to determine at what age infants demonstrate sensitivity to word order. She presented 10- and 14-month-old babies with sentences, some of which had normal English word order; others had scrambled word order. The 14-month-olds, but not the 10-month-olds, preferred listening to the sentences with normal word order. It is, thus, highly probable that children set this parameter before they produce any words at all.

Children with SLI also do not make errors of word order. Word order errors are a feature neither of early speech nor of SLI speech. As mentioned earlier in this book, Goldin-Meadow and Mylander (1990) discovered ordering preferences in the "home signs" of deaf children who had never been exposed to language. Word order may be one of the most basic structural features of human language and, as such, should be very salient for the language-learning child. Positive evidence for this parameter is available in the speech of the environment from the very beginning. All a child must do is hear a sentence in which the verb precedes its object to know that his is a head-first language. Pinker's (1984) semantic bootstrapping hypothesis suggests that subjects, verbs, and objects are initially acquired when the child maps them onto events in the environment.

Because English is a language with very strict word order in its sentences, the few constructions in which the standard word order is altered are very difficult for children. One such construction is the *passive*, in which the object of the verb is actually moved to the front, as in "The cat was stroked by the child." As suggested previously, the underlying form (or D-Structure) of sentences must have the object following the verb, but in the case of the passive it moves into the specifier of IP and serves as the subject of the sentence, leaving a trace (t) behind, following the verb. The morphology of the passive is different from any other construction; it has an auxiliary (a form of the verb *to* be—in this sentence *was*—and the participle form of the verb). Thus, it is a very complicated structure, even though it is technically a simple sentence because it has only one verb.

English-speaking children (including those with SLI) produce very few full passive sentences, although they do produce truncated passives such as "The dog was chased" or the more common "The dog got chased" (Horgan, 1978). It is not clear exactly what kind of an analysis the child has of these structures. It may be that the child is using the participle form of the verb as sort of an adjective, similar to "The dog was black." In studies of children's comprehension of full passives, it has been observed by many psycholinguists (e.g., Strohner & Nelson, 1974) that children interpret such sentences as though they were following standard word order. Thus, "The cat was chased by the dog" is interpreted as meaning that the cat chased the dog. This is an excellent example of a very general feature of children's interpretation of sentences. If the sentence instantiates a structure the child does not yet command in his grammar, he will analyze it using structures that he does have available to him. It is entirely possible that the mismatch of immature analyses with more advanced structures is an important source of information and positive evidence for the young child. In our example, for instance, when "The cat was chased by the dog" is analyzed as "The cat chased the dog," there is an auxiliary (*was*) and a preposition (*by*) that do not match the analysis. A further source of evidence for the child would be provided if there was an event in the world (or in a book) in which the dog was doing the chasing. Children do not learn language from decontextualized sentences. They must analyze them in many cases as having meanings that match events occurring in the world around them.

A continuing theme in this book is that we want to be able to evaluate the child's underlying grammar, whenever possible, independent of his ability to produce and understand particular structures. This is of particular interest in the case of the passive construction, because children use it relatively late. Some children with SLI seem never to use the construction. A very clever technique for determining whether children have a grammar that describes passive sentences despite the fact that they rarely use them is the elicited production task. In this task, the child is shown an action by a set of toys—say, a pig chases a cow. The child is asked "Tell me what happened to the cow. The cow . . . ," and the child is invited to complete the sentence.

Smith-Lock (1993) used this technique in the study mentioned previously and demonstrated that children with SLI who do not spontaneously produce full passives can do so in the elicited production task. What was of particular interest in her data was that the children with SLI made many errors on the passive morphology, while getting the basic structure right. The following are some examples of the passive constructions: "It's gonna be ride" and "The tree got knocked over from the baby." Smith-Lock pointed out that the passives of the children with SLI are syntactically correct, but the children have a great deal of trouble with the morphology of the passive construction. As in the morphological component of the study, mentioned previously, the children with SLI performed similarly to the language-matched control group and much worse than the age-matched control group. This reinforces the belief that children with SLI are developing language in a similar manner, though much more slowly, than are normally developing children.

Question Formation

Having introduced the basic sentence structure in Figures 4.1 and 4.2, I can talk about question formation in a more theoretically interesting way than I did in the last chapter. When a child produces a yes–no question (e.g., "Is the kitty chasing the bunny?" or "Did the kitty chase the bunny?"), it is of great significance because it means that he is producing a structure that requires movement and that he is moving the auxiliary into the complementizer position. Similarly, the production of *wh–* questions with inverted auxiliaries demonstrates movement into the specifier position of CP (see Figure 4.5). Thus, there can be no question that children who are producing such structures are using all the available functional categories of basic sentence structure.

As stated previously, early yes–no questions are of the form "Daddy going?" and early *wh–* questions are of the form "Where Daddy going?" An important question is whether the child who uses these forms has a grammar that does not allow movement, or whether there is simply nothing to move since the auxiliary and modal systems have not developed. The latter analysis is preferable for theoretical reasons, because of Continuity Theory. We want to analyze child grammars at every stage as conforming to Universal Grammar, and UG does allow movement. Empirically, this position seems the best, also. It seems that as soon as the auxiliary and modal systems develop, inversion in yes–no questions begins so that the child who said "Daddy going?" now says "Is Daddy going?" or "Can Daddy go?" Many children, however, produce wh– questions without inversion, so the same child might produce "Is Daddy going?" but "Who kitty is chasing?" Weinberg (1990) reviewed many production studies of this period of language development and demonstrated that some children begin inversion in yes–no and wh– questions at the same time and some invert first in yes–no questions. However, no children invert in wh– questions before doing so in yes–no questions.

Another very interesting aspect of wh– movement revolves around the fact that there are complex constraints on movement in all languages (such constraints are part of UG). The example of wh– movement given in Figure 4.6 is local movement; an element moves within a single clause. However, wh– questions can move elements from a deeply embedded clause, such as "Whom$_i$ did John know that Sally believed that Jane loved t_i?" (The way this structure would look is that each embedded clause would be the complement of the higher verb, with *that* occupying the complementizer positions.) This is called *long-distance* movement, and there is no limit to the distance a wh– word can move. However, there are structural constraints on long-distance movement. For instance, it is ungrammatical to say "Whom$_i$ did John pet the cat that chased t_i?" (answer being "the mouse"). Because these constraints are part of UG, children should obey them from the very beginning. Although children do not produce such sentences, we know that simply because a structure is not produced, we cannot be sure it is ungrammatical for a child.

De Villiers and Roeper (1990; de Villiers, Roeper, & Vainikka, 1990; Roeper & de Villiers, 1992) devised a clever technique to test whether children ages 3 years, 5 months, to 6 years allowed wh– movement that should be ruled out by UG. They developed a pictured story such as the following: "A little boy is playing outside and he falls out of a tree and hurts his arm. When he is having a bath, he discovers the bruise on his arm and says to his father, 'I must have hurt myself when I fell this afternoon.'" The child is then asked the question, "When did the boy say he hurt himself?" It is grammatical for the word *when* to refer either to when the boy did the telling or to when he hurt his arm. There is no restriction on long-distance movement in this sentence; *when* could have been moved from either the earlier sentence, "The boy said . . . ," or the later one, "He hurt himself . . . ." Children were willing to interpret such questions either way; that is, they answered either "When he was taking his bath" or "When he was playing this afternoon." However, when the question was formulated in such a way that long-distance movement would not be grammatical, as in "When did he say how he hurt himself?" the children answered only as though *how* went with *say*, giving the answer "When he was having his bath." They did not answer this question with *when* relating to *hurt* and did not say "When he was playing this afternoon." Roeper and de Villiers took the fact that the children answered the short-distance question more often in the second kind of question than in the first as an indication that they knew that the long-distance question was ungrammatical. This was the result for the overwhelming number of their subjects. The weight of empirical evidence, then, converges on the theoretically desirable claim that children never have grammars that violate constraints on movement.

Relative Clauses

The structure of relative clauses is closely related to that of *wh–* questions, because in both a moved element (a *wh–* word or a relative pronoun) is coindexed with a trace. In the sentence, "The doctor set the leg that the man broke," "that the man broke" is the relative clause. A trace in object position, the relative pronoun, and the NP that is relativized all are coindexed, since they all refer to the same thing ("the leg"). Figure 4.7 presents the phrase marker describing the structure of this sentence. The meaning of a relative clause is clear. It modifies the NP that is relativized and also tells which one (of many such things) is being talked about. In the sentence above, the relative clause tells which leg the doctor set. For this reason, such a construction is called a *restrictive* relative clause.

The first thing to ask about relative clauses is whether children's early grammars will create them. Crain, McKee, and Emiliani (1990) with Italian-speaking subjects and McKee, McDaniel, and Snedeker (1994) with 2- and 3-year-old English-speaking children used an elicited production task that demonstrated that children do indeed

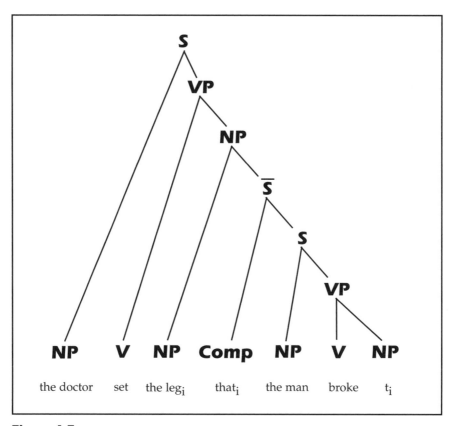

Figure 4.7

have grammars that create relative clauses. The technique was the following: There are two experimenters and a set of small toys. One experimenter, the storyteller, told the subject a story using toys as props while the second experimenter watched. The story was always about at least two identical objects, one of which was performing some action (e.g., two identical lions, one of whom was jumping on a table). After the story was enacted, the second experimenter hid her eyes and the storyteller whispered to the child to tell the second experimenter which toy to pick up, after the blindfold was removed. The storyteller always indicated the toy that had performed the action in the story. When the blindfold was removed, it was pragmatically appropriate and communicatively effective for the child to say something such as

"Pick up the lion that jumped on the table." All the children in this experiment produced relative clauses, indicating that they had grammars of sufficient maturity to construct them. Although all produced the correct structures, some used *what* as the relative pronoun, as in "Touch the boy what jumped up and down."

Relative clauses, which appear often in standardized tests as examples of complex sentences and are used often by experimenters to investigate subjects' syntactic skills, are particularly interesting because they reveal the complex interplay of competence and performance. Research on the interpretation of relative clauses also gives us some very good ideas about how to create materials in our work with children that will maximize our ability to evaluate their grammars and remove extraneous performance factors.

The earliest work on relative clauses was done by Sheldon (1974), who investigated children's comprehension of the following kinds of relative clauses, using an act-out task.

- *Subject–Subject* (SS): In this type of relative clause, the subject NP is relativized and the relativized element is the subject of the embedded clause, as in "The cow that kissed the pig hugged the sheep."

- *Subject–Object* (SO): In this type of relative clause, the subject NP is relativized and the relativized element is the object of the embedded clause, as in "The cow that the pig kissed hugged the sheep."

- *Object–Object* (OO): In this type of relative clause, the object NP is relativized and the relativized element is the object of the embedded clause, as in "The cow kissed the pig that the sheep hugged."

- *Object–Subject* (OS): In this type of relative clause, the object NP is relativized and the relativized element is the subject of the embedded clause, as in "The cow kissed the pig that hugged the sheep."

Sheldon found that children performed best on SS and OO relatives, and she developed the Parallel Function Hypothesis. It was that the relative clause will be easier to interpret if the relativized element plays the same grammatical role in both the matrix (the main) and the embedded (the relative) clauses. Although further research did not always confirm Sheldon's hypothesis, her work formed the basis of much later work that investigates the relative difficulty of the various types of relative clauses.

All four of these sentence types have the same relative clause structure described at the beginning of this section, so they do not differ from one another from the point of view of the grammatical rules that underlie them. However, they do differ in difficulty for reasons having to do with their differential ease of processing. Sentence processing is, of course, a function of the child's linguistic performance, rather than linguistic competence. Let us consider what aspects of these sentences could make some of them more difficult (or easier) to process than others. In both the SS and SO sentences, the relative clause intervenes between the subject of the main clause and its verb ("The cow" and "hugged" in the above examples). This requires the hearer to hold the main clause subject in working memory while the relative clause is being processed, then recover it to continue processing the rest of the sentence. The memory difficulty should hold equally for SS and SO sentences, but there is another factor to consider. Children (and adults, as well) process sentences much more easily if they conform to standard subject–verb–object word order than if they contain an element that has been moved out of standard order (as in passive sentences.) The SS sentence has the advantage that both the main clause and the embedded clause are in standard subject–verb–object word order. This has the effect that the first NP is the subject of both clauses. The SO, on the other hand, has the double disadvantage that the main clause is interrupted and the embedded clause is out of standard word order. Because the object is relativized, "that the pig kissed" is in object–subject–verb order. Most studies show that the SO is the most difficult kind of relative clause. On the other hand, SS relatives are artificially easy, because the child can simply take the first NP to be the subject of both verbs. Thus, he can correctly interpret the sentence without having to use his grammar to figure out its structure.

In the OO relative clause, the main clause is not interrupted; however, the embedded clause does have the elements out of standard word order. The OS sentence is the most "pure" kind of relative clause sentence. The child must "unravel" the relative clause to know what the sentence means, but it has no other properties (interruption or nonstandard word order) that would make it difficult to process. It is, then, the best kind of relative clause sentence to use if you want to test a child's ability to process relative clauses. The difficulty of processing a sentence with a clause embedded between the subject and the verb, or one that is out of standard word order, is a result of the child's developing sentence processing abilities. There are, therefore, linguistic properties of sentences that can impede the child's ability to use his underlying grammar (competence) to assign structure to a sentence that he hears.

Tavakolian (1981) used an act-out task to investigate children's interpretation of OS sentences. She found that a typical error children make when they misinterpret OS sentences such as "The cow kissed the pig that jumped over the fence" is that they make the cow kiss the pig and jump over the fence. She suggested that such children are interpreting the sentence as having a coordinated structure, rather than an embedded structure. Psycholinguists believe that coordinated structures are easier to process, for both children and adults, than are subordinated structures, so it is plausible to suppose that young children would misanalyze an embedded structure as coordinated. Tavakolian called this the Coordinated Structure Hypothesis.

It is reasonable, on the one hand, to suppose that a coordinated structure would be easier to process than an embedded one. However, recent work investigating children's interpretation of coordinated sentences (Cairns, McDaniel, Hsu, DeFino, & Konstantyn, in press) has shown that 4- and 5-year-old children often do not assign the same interpretation to coordinated sentences as adults do. Some children report that in a sentence such as "The horse kissed the pig and jumped over the fence" either the horse or the pig could be jumping. Some also allow the cow, who is not mentioned in the sentence, to be jumping. These findings about the interpretation of coordinated structures make the Coordinated Structure Hypothesis questionable as an explanation of why children make the error described in the previous paragraph on OS sentences. It probably is the case that coordinated sentences are easier to process than relative clauses or any embedded structures, but their interpretation does not seem to be as Tavakolian (1981) would have assumed. A great deal more work needs to be done on coordinated sentences, their structure and interpretation in children's grammars.

Goodluck and Tavakolian (1982) further investigated children's interpretation of OS relative clauses and identified yet another property of relative clause sentences that can make them difficult to process. They gave children OS sentences of the following types:

1. Sentences with three animate NPs, such as "The horse kicked the cow that pushed the sheep."

2. Sentences with two animate and one inanimate NP, such as "The horse kicked the cow that pushed the gate."

3. Sentences with only two animate NPs, such as "The horse kicked the cow that jumped up and down."

The subjects, who were 4- and 5-year-old children, performed best on the third kind of sentence (with 76% correct), next best on the second (70% correct), and worst on the first type with three animate NPs (50% correct). It is easy to see why sentence 1 should be harder than sentence 3, because the former is longer and has an object in the embedded clause. However, why should sentence 2 be easier than sentence 1? Both have embedded objects, and they are of equal length. Sentence 2 is easier because children have a clear preference for subjects to be animate and objects to be inanimate.

Chapman and Kohn (1977) demonstrated the preference of preschool children for animate subjects and inanimate objects. Even though the children used their grammatical knowledge of English word order to interpret sentences such as "The boy kissed the girl" correctly, they performed more poorly on sentences with inanimate subjects and animate objects such as "The boat bumped the boy" than they did on sentences with animate subjects and inanimate objects such as "The boy pulled the boat." This phenomenon is probably related to something I discuss in more detail in the next chapter, which is the *thematic role* played by various elements of a sentence. In "The boy pulled the boat," the boy is the *agent* (that is his thematic role). However, in "The boat bumped the boy," the boat is not acting of its own volition, so it is not an agent. It is a theme or perhaps an *instrument* (someone else is using the boat to bump the boy). Thus, children's preference for animacy is probably more properly characterized as a preference for subjects to be agents.

In an experiment I once conducted on children's interpretation of relative clauses, I wanted to use all four types of relative clauses. Furthermore, following Goodluck and Tavakolian (1982), I wanted to make my sentences easy by including only two animate NPs. This goal required me to construct an OO sentence of the following type: "The cow kissed the sheep that the gate bumped." My children performed terribly on that sentence, much worse than they usually do on OO relatives, compared with the other types. I finally figured out what I had done wrong: My embedded clause with the object relativized had an inanimate subject and an animate object.

Hamburger and Crain (1982) discovered yet another factor influencing children's performance on relative clause sentences that has nothing to do with any linguistic property of the sentences themselves. The semantics of a restricted relative clause is to single out one object from a set of such objects. That is why the elicited production task developed by Crain, McKee, and Emiliani (1990) and McKee et al. (1994) worked; it required the child to identify one of two identical characters to the blindfolded experimenter. This is a *pragmatic* requirement of a sentence with a restricted relative clause—that it select among identical characters. If an experimenter asks a child to act out the sentence "The cow kissed the pig that jumped up and down" and there is only one pig in the toy set, then the sentence is pragmatically very odd. According to Hamburger and Crain, such a sentence is "infelicitous." Indeed, they demonstrated that children perform much better if the array of toys includes at least two of the relativized characters. This is a single example of a very important point one must keep in mind in all kinds of work with children. The things we ask them to do must make sense and must be pragmatically plausible. This is true in experimental situations, as well as in testing and therapeutic contexts. Sentences do not exist in isolation in the real world. If we are testing or teaching properties of individual sentences, we need to provide as much context as we can to make the sentence pragmatically appropriate, without making it artificially easier to process.

One of the few good intervention studies in the literature was done by Roth (1979, 1984), who used two different techniques to teach children to understand relative clause structures. The sentences were of all four types described previously, and each had three animate noun phrases. Her subjects were children 3 1/2 to 4 1/2 years of age, who did not perform well on a pretest of their abilities to interpret sentences with relative clauses, using an act-out task. One intervention group was trained by the experimenter's demonstrating for the children (using small toys) the interpretation of sentences with relative clauses. The other group was trained by the experimenter's separating each sentence explicitly into two simple sentences and demonstrating the meaning of each. Both groups improved equally, going from 16% correct on the pretest to over 40% after training, and performed significantly better on a posttest than did a control group that received no instruction. Roth returned after 2 weeks, administered another posttest, and demonstrated that the children in the two intervention groups had improved further in their ability to interpret sentences with relative clauses; they performed correctly more than 50% of the time.

What was the reason for the success of Roth's intervention? Recall that the studies by Crain, McKee, and Emiliani (1990) and McKee et al. (1994) elicited relative clauses from children as young (and younger) than Roth's subjects. So perhaps Roth's subjects were not actually acquiring the grammar of relative clauses, but were acquiring the ability to use that grammar to interpret them. Whether Roth was observing changes in competence or in performance, intervention studies are of great importance for our understanding of the relationship between children's language development and their language experience. Such studies are highly relevant to decisions about the design of therapeutic intervention for children with language disorders.

Binding Principles

Pronouns are of great interest to linguists and psycholinguists because they represent perfectly the intersection between linguistic competence and linguistic performance. Consider the referent of *he* in a sentence such as "He said that John was tired." There is a principle of grammar that prevents *he* from referring to *John*, but there is no principle of grammar that will indicate to whom *he* does refer. That is a decision to be made by the hearer of the sentence, based on the topic of conversation, the nonlinguistic as well as the linguistic context. In the sentence "John said that he was tired," there is no grammatical restriction on the reference of *he*. It can refer to John or to any male in the discourse context. The grammar, then, in some circumstances constrains the referent of pronouns; the performance system determines their reference within the constraints of the grammar. The situation is different, however, in the case of reflexive pronouns; the grammar determines their reference.

The grammatical principles relating to the interpretation of pronouns are called the *binding principles*. These principles are considered to be part of Universal Grammar, and apply (with aspects of language-particular variation) to pronominal elements in all languages of the world. Study of these principles has consumed a vast literature in the recent past and relates to a great variety of pronominal elements in English and other languages. The description given here of the binding principles is greatly simplified, but adequate to understand the research that is being done on children's obedience to these principles. Because these principles are part of UG and are of fundamental importance to even the simplest of sentences, they constitute a feature of child language that has been studied extensively. The research has extended to many child languages other than English, but I restrict this discussion to English.

Principle A of the Binding Theory refers to all *anaphors*, but is restricted in this text to *reflexive pronouns*. Although other anaphors, such as *reciprocals* (*each other*) have been studied in research with children (Otsu, 1981), the vast majority of work has been done with reflexives. Principle A states that reflexives must be locally bound. It accounts for why sentences such as "Grover patted himself" must mean that Grover patted Grover. To understand what binding means, we need to understand the structural principle of *c-command*, a very simple property of sentence structure that plays a role in a great many linguistic processes. Consider Figure 4.8 in which the sentence "Grover patted himself" is diagrammed. (Notice that the simpler version of sentence structure is used because we do not need to refer to the functional nodes IP and CP.) In this sentence, the NP *Grover* c-commands the NP *himself*. This is because one NP c-commands another if the branching node immediately above the first dominates the second. You can figure out the c-command relationship using your finger. Put your finger on the *Grover* NP; move it up to the next branching node, which is the S, then move your finger down the lines of the tree diagram until you get to the *himself* NP. The fact that you can do this demonstrates that the S node dominates the *himself* NP, and therefore the *Grover* NP c-commands the *himself* NP.

Now we are in a position to understand the definition of *bound*. It means coindexed with a c-commanding NP. The requirement that the reflexive be "locally bound" means that it must be coindexed with a c-commanding NP within its clause. (This would be within a simple

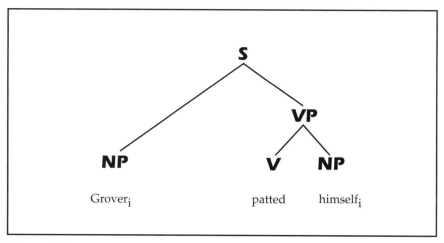

Figure 4.8

sentence or within a sentence that is embedded in a larger one.) I described coindexing when I discussed movement processes. A *wh*–
word was coindexed with its trace to indicate that they refer to the
same thing. Similarly, a relative pronoun was coindexed to its trace.
Principle A says, then, that in a structure such as that in Figure 4.8,
Grover and *himself* must be coindexed. It follows, then, that they must
corefer; that is, they must refer to each other. Consider the structure of
the two-clause sentence "Ernie said that Grover patted himself," described in Figure 4.9. *Grover* and *himself* must be bound, by Principle
A, but since *Grover* must be only locally bound, it cannot be bound by
Ernie, which is outside its clause. Thus, the sentence cannot mean that
Ernie said that Grover patted Ernie.

Although Principle A is operative in all human languages, they
differ in how the term *local* is defined. Some languages, such as
English, define all clauses as local, whether or not they are tensed. So
himself must be *Grover* in "Ernie wanted Grover to pat himself" (which
has the infinitive, untensed form of the verb) as well as in "Ernie said
that Grover patted himself." There are other languages, however, in
which local means only tensed clauses, so *himself* could refer to either
Ernie or Grover in "Ernie wanted Grover to pat himself." Given our
Principles and Parameters theory of language and language acquisition, a child should develop a grammar in which Principle A is oper-

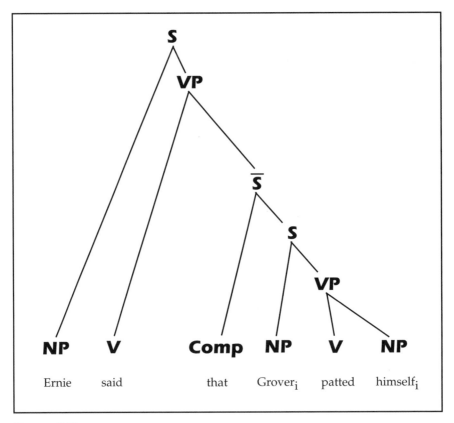

Figure 4.9

ative as soon as he learns which words are reflexives. The definition of local varies parametrically, so he will have to receive positive evidence to know that in English the domain of application of Principle A is all clauses, whether or not they are tensed.

 Principle B is essentially a mirror image of Principle A. It says that personal pronouns, such as *him* and *her,* must not be coindexed with a c-commanding NP in the local domain. Such pronouns cannot be locally bound; they must be free. Thus, in a structure such as that in Figure 4.10, showing the structure of the sentence "Grover hit him," *Grover* and *him* must be contraindexed. We show this by giving *him* an i index and *Grover* a j index. In the complex sentence "Ernie said that Grover hit him" (Figure 4.11), *Ernie* can bind *him,* because it is outside

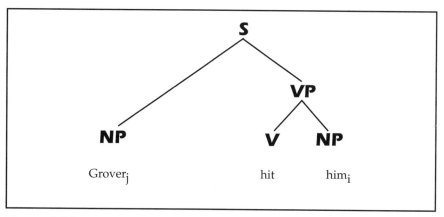

Figure 4.10

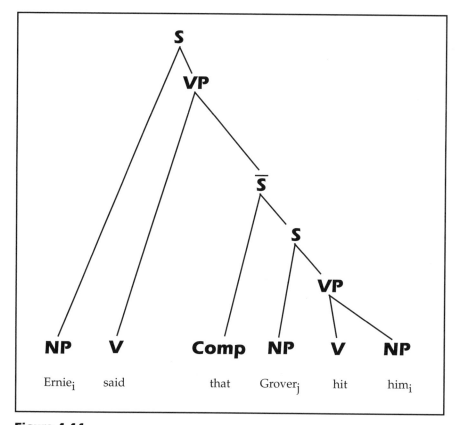

Figure 4.11

the local clausal domain, but *Grover* cannot. Principle B was originally designed to account for why adults do not allow *him* to refer to *Grover* in either of the sentences above. Under ordinary circumstances, NPs that are contraindexed do not corefer.

Although the grammar places constraints on the reference of pronouns, as stated previously, it never requires that they refer to an element in the sentence. The referent of *him* in "Grover hit him" or in "Ernie says that Grover hit him" is completely dependent upon non-linguistic factors. The hearer of the sentence will select a referent either from the discourse context or from the situational context. Pronominal reference in most languages (except in the case of reflexives) is not governed by linguistic rules. It is a completely psycholinguistic activity, governed by pragmatic and discourse factors.

Principle C of the binding theory has the entailment (which is sufficient for our purposes) that a pronoun cannot be coindexed with any NP that it c-commands. It is completely general and applies to all contexts, not only local clausal ones. Thus, in Figure 4.12, which illustrates the structure of the sentence "He patted Grover," *he* and *Grover* must be contraindexed. *He* must be contraindexed with both *Ernie* and *Grover* in "He said that Ernie patted Grover" (Figure 4.13). Again, in general, contraindexing indicates noncoreference; thus, for adults, *he* must refer to someone in the discourse context, but neither *Ernie* nor *Grover*.

Binding Principles in the Grammars of Young Children

If we assume that the binding principles are part of Universal Grammar, then as soon as children learn to classify lexical items as reflexives, personal pronouns, and NPs to which pronouns can refer, they should be able to apply the binding principles. This is a combination of Pinker's (1984) Continuity Theory, which says that children's grammars will always conform to Universal Grammar, and Wexler and Chien's (1985) Lexical Learning Hypothesis, which says that children must learn lexical items before they can apply principles of UG. The important point here is that, because the binding principles are part of Universal Grammar, they are, according to the nativist theory of language acquisition, part of the LAD and do not have to be learned. The child is biologically prepared to acquire a grammar that will incorporate these principles. In fact, it would be impossible for the

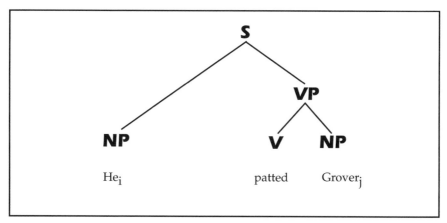

Figure 4.12

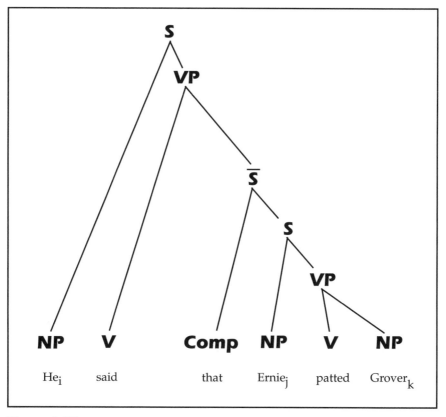

Figure 4.13

child to learn the principles based solely on positive evidence (as discussed previously). The child must end up with the knowledge that "Grover patted himself" is a grammatical sentence of English, but that it is not grammatical with the meaning that Grover patted anyone else. To acquire this knowledge by negative evidence, every English-speaking child would have to use such a sentence with the meaning that Grover patted someone other than himself, be corrected, and respond to the correction by making a change in his grammar. Furthermore, as I discuss in a moment, this would have to happen to every child by the age of 4. This scenario is obviously false. Therefore, we have identified a feature of grammar that children can learn using inborn information about the form of human language that they could not have learned from experience.

A great deal of research has been done on the acquisition of all three binding principles. In general, it appears that Principle A is acquired very early, certainly by the age of 4. Actually, instead of speaking of the principle as being acquired, we should say that children demonstrate obedience to the principle, allowing us to assume that they have classified reflexives as the kind of word to which Principle A refers (Chien & Wexler, 1990; Grodzinsky & Kave, 1993/1994; McDaniel, Cairns, & Hsu, 1990). McDaniel et al. showed that in a judgment task very young children will allow a reflexive to refer to a character not mentioned in the sentence. They enacted possible interpretations using small toys and asked the children if the enactments matched the sentence. Some children (all younger than 4 years, 1 month) allowed "Grover hit himself" to mean that Grover hit Ernie. (Chien & Wexler, 1990, reported a similar finding for their young subjects.) All older children obeyed Principle A by reporting that reflexives could not refer outside the sentence.

It is well known that young children say *hisself* instead of *himself*. This is an overgeneralization of the pattern including *herself, myself,* and *ourselves,* all of which consist of the possessive pronoun and *self.* McDaniel et al. (1990) suggested that when children are very young they actually interpret the reflexives as a possessive and the word *self.* It is only later that a child realizes *himself* is a reflexive and not "his self." This constitutes the lexical learning that results in the child's consistent obedience to Principle A.

What the child must learn, with respect to Principles A and B, is the local domain selected by his language. Recall that some languages (e.g., English) define local domain as all clauses, tensed or untensed. Some other languages, however, require a reflexive to be bound within tensed clauses, but allow it to refer outside untensed ones (although not outside the sentence). All children can learn all languages, so we must assume that all children begin with the same acquisition strategy. Furthermore, it must be a strategy that will allow children in either type of language to end up with the correct local domain, based only on positive evidence. Keeping this in mind, let us try to figure out what children's first hypothesis should be about the local domain. Should their first hypothesis be that the reflexive cannot refer outside any clause—or only outside tensed ones? Suppose the child begins with the hypothesis that the reflexive cannot refer outside any clause (tensed or untensed). If he is going to learn English, he will be in luck, because his initial hypothesis will be correct. If, on the other hand, he is learning a language that allows reflexives to refer outside untensed clauses, that will be okay, too, because he will hear sentences in that language such as "Mommy asked Daddy to help herself." That will constitute positive evidence that reflexives can (in his non-English language) refer outside untensed clauses.

However, what if the first hypothesis were the other way around? Suppose children start off thinking that the reflexive can refer outside untensed clauses. The child learning the non-English language would be fine, because he would be right about his language. However, the child learning English would be in big trouble, because his grammar would generate "Mommy asked Daddy to help herself" as a well-formed sentence and would allow *himself* to refer to either Grover or Ernie in the sentence "Ernie wanted Grover to pat himself." If the child had such a grammar, he would never be able to discover by positive evidence that he is wrong. He would never hear a sentence such as "Mommy asked Daddy to help herself," but neither would he reliably receive correction on the (probably rare) occasions when he would use such a sentence (which would be negative evidence). Thus, our learnability principle that the child receives only positive evidence leads us to predict that the child's first hypothesis about the local domain for the application of Principles A and B will be that it is both tensed and untensed clauses and that reflexives cannot refer outside of either. This prediction has been tested, with less than positive results.

Solan (1987) investigated the domain issue with respect to

Principle A and found that children aged 4 to 7 make more errors with the reflexive in untensed clauses (24% in sentences such as "Ernie wanted Grover to pat himself") than in tensed ones (only 8% in sentences such as "Ernie said that Grover would pat himself"). Solan suggested that such children had set the domain of Principle A incorrectly, but acknowledged this as presenting a learnability problem. The McDaniel et al. (1990) experiment on the binding principles in child English included sentences to test whether children obeyed the correct local domain for the application of Principle A. All children who knew that *himself* was a reflexive obeyed the local domain and restricted reference of himself to Ernie in the sentence "Grover said that Ernie patted himself." Contrary to the expectation based on learnability considerations, however, one child (of 20) in their first study and three children (of 19) in their second also allowed the reflexive to refer to the matrix subject (Grover) in a sentence such as "Grover wants Ernie to touch himself." In a larger study of 63 much older, third-grade, children, Waltzman (1994; Waltzman & Cairns, 1995) found 12 children who allowed the supposedly non-English interpretation that *himself* could refer to either Grover or Ernie.

The existence of such children is a puzzle; we cannot figure out how they can ever learn to restrict the domain given only positive evidence. One possibility that some linguists have considered is that the English language is changing with respect to the domain of application of Principle A. It is also possible that some people reach adulthood with the domain set in this way, so their grammars constitute a slightly different dialect of English. Such a state of affairs would surely not present a person with any serious communication problems. There are adults (I am one of them) with less definite judgments about the grammaticality of sentences such as "John wanted Sally to scratch himself" than about "*John said that Sally scratched himself." Imagine a scenario in which John has a mosquito bite that he can't reach, so Sally scratches it for him. It would be barely possible (for me) to say "John wanted Sally to scratch himself" but, afterward, not "John said that Sally scratched himself." (How do you feel about those sentences?) In an important study of Principle A involving both normal and SLI subjects, Franks and Connell (in press) found that the children with language impairments performed similarly to the normal controls. Furthermore, they seemed to have fewer problems with the domain of Principle A than did the normally developing subjects.

Research on Principle B has revealed one of the greatest puzzles in language acquisition. Many studies (e.g., Chien & Wexler, 1990;

McDaniel et al., 1990; Wexler & Chien, 1985) have shown that children disobey Principle B until they are very old. For their study Chien and Wexler designed a "Simon Says" game, in which the child subject was asked to obey the directions of the puppet (who was the same gender as the child). Children aged 2 years, 6 months, through 6 years, 6 months, were given sentences such as "Kitty (the puppet) says that Sarah (the child) should point to her." In every age group, a substantial number of the children responded by pointing to themselves, in violation of Principle B. There was no improvement with age (as there was in the component of their study testing Principle A). In fact, the oldest group violated Principle B 36% of the time. Using their judgment task McDaniel et al. identified 11 (of 20) 4- and 5-year-old children who said that, if Grover was patting himself, it would be fine to describe that event with the sentence "Grover is patting him." This was true even if another male character (Ernie) was present in the discourse space. It is important to note that the children never required *him* to refer to Grover; they said it can refer either to Grover or to Ernie. Thus, it is not as though they are confusing the personal pronoun with a reflexive pronoun. It is simply that they allow coreference, which is ruled out by adults. In the Waltzman (1994; Waltzman & Cairns, 1995) study of 63 third graders, 63% failed to obey Principle B. At this point in the research of this question, we do not even know at what age children finally "grow up." The Waltzman study had the oldest group that has been investigated to date. We need to know the age beyond which all children respond like adults. Unlike the issue with respect to the domain of Principle A, there is no variation of adult judgment with respect to Principle B. Experiments typically include adult subjects, who obey Principle B consistently. In years of teaching and speaking to groups of people about these issues, I have found only one adult who felt it was okay to say "Grover hit him" if Grover is hitting Grover.

What is going on here? Why do even very old children, whose grammars seem to be adultlike in every other respect, appear to disobey Principle B? I present a number of possibilities, but there is not one that all psycholinguists agree upon. It is an area of intense research and debate. The first question to ask is, are children disobeying Principle B because it is not operative in their grammar? If this were the case, it would mean that in a sentence such as "Grover hit him," the child is coindexing, rather than contraindexing, *Grover* and *him* ("*Grover$_i$ hit him$_i$"). If so, it would be fairly dramatic disconfirmation of Pinker's (1984) Continuity Theory, which is the hypothesis that early child grammars conform to UG. Chien and Wexler (1990) thought of a very clever way to approach this question. To understand their test of whether children violate this principle by coindexing, let us first consider an example of a reflexive, in which coindexing is not only allowed, but required. The sentence "Every cow is scratching herself" means that there are a number of cows, and the first cow is scratching herself, the second cow is scratching herself, and so on. This is called a *distributed* interpretation, and it is possible only if *every cow* and *herself* are coindexed. Wexler and Chien (1985) realized that if a child were violating Principle B by coindexing *every cow* and *her* in the sentence "Every cow is scratching her," then he would allow the distributed interpretation, in which the first cow scratches herself, the second cow scratches herself, and so on. But the children did not do this. Many children who allow "The cow is scratching her" to mean that the cow is scratching herself will not give the distributed interpretation to "Every cow is scratching her." (This finding has been verified by other researchers, such as McDaniel et al., 1990.) Thus, Wexler and Chien argued that the children know Principle B and are not ungrammatically coindexing *the cow* and *her*. Their hypothesis was that the children are contraindexing the name and the pronoun, in accord with Principle B, but they are allowing coreference despite contraindexing, which is very unusual for adults. According to this argument, then, it is not Principle B that the children fail to know; it is, instead, a nonlinguistic rule that contraindexing usually implies noncoreference. This is a nice idea, since it saves Continuity Theory. It says that children and adults share Principle B of the binding theory; it does not, however, help us much in understanding what it is that adults have, but children lack.

Many linguists and psycholinguists are attempting to solve the problem of how children can finally grow up to have the adult judgments with respect to sentences such as "The cow is scratching her." In doing so, the researchers begin by observing under what circumstances adults will allow coreference between an NP and a personal pronoun despite the contraindexing required by Principle B. This occurs most often in the first person and always serves a pragmatic purpose of some sort. A well-known example (originally attributed to the linguist George Lakeoff) is "I dreamed I was Brigitte Bardot, and then I kissed me." Coreference between the contraindexed *I* and *me* conveys a subtly different message than would have been conveyed by *myself.* So the conclusion is that adults can use coreference despite contraindexing under certain (highly restricted) pragmatic circumstances, which Chien and Wexler (1990) called simply *Principle P*. Children, lacking Principle P, hear adults using coreference despite contraindexing, assume it is an acceptable thing to do, and allow it when asked in psycholinguistic experiments. There is some evidence that children do not violate Principle B in their own speech. Bloom, Barss, Nicol, and Conway (1994) examined the use of pronouns by three children between the ages of 2 and 5 from the CHILDES database and found no disobedience to Principle B in their productions. Thus, according to Chien and Wexler's hypothesis, children know Principle B, but they must learn Principle P. We have now replaced one learnability puzzle with another. What is Principle P, and how do children acquire it without positive evidence?

A hypothesis first suggested by McDaniel et al. (1990) and tested by McDaniel and Maxfield (1992) represents a helpful step in the attempt to discover what children must learn in order to behave like adults with respect to Principle B. They noted that in adult speech, apparent B violations (in which a noun is allowed to corefer with a contraindexed personal pronoun for pragmatic purposes) are accompanied by *contrastive stress*. Suppose a person is a candidate for some office and is asked whom she plans to vote for. She might say, "I'm going to vote for myself," or she might say, "I'm going to vote for ME." (Stress is indicated by capital letters.) This would be a case of coreference despite contraindexing and would convey a slightly different effect than would the sentence with the reflexive. She would not, however, say, "I'm going to vote for me" without using contrastive stress on the pronoun. Contrastive stress is a pragmatic device that is used for emphasis ("Pass the PEAS"). McDaniel and her colleagues suggested that it is also used to signal coreference despite contraindexing. Now, suppose a child has not yet learned the pragmatic use of contrastive stress. He would hear someone say, "I'm going to vote for ME" and would assume that (regardless of stress) it is okay to have coreference between contraindexed NPs in certain pragmatic situations. Thus, the child who doesn't know about contrastive stress will assume that such coreference is acceptable without stress in those pragmatic contexts.

McDaniel and Maxfield (1992) suggested, therefore, it is the pragmatic use of contrastive stress that children must learn about. Their hypothesized developmental sequence goes like this. First, the child knows Principle B, but does not know how the pragmatic device of contrastive stress works. When adults use contrastive stress to signal coreference despite contraindexing, the child doesn't realize that the coreference must be signaled by contrastive stress. Such children will assume coreference is possible without stress, and they will appear to disobey Principle B in experiments. Next, the child learns that contrastive stress is used pragmatically for emphasis. Now he will be able to recognize contrastive stress in the speech of the adults in the environment and can detect that coreference despite contraindexing is signaled by contrastively stressing the pronoun. Such a child will no longer appear to violate Principle B in experiments. He will judge as inappropriate sentences such as "Grover scratched him" in which Grover is scratching himself and *him* is unstressed.

To test their hypothesis, McDaniel and Maxfield designed a contrastive stress test to determine whether the 37 children in their experiment (ages 3 years, 1 month, to 6 years, 10 months) were sensitive to contrastive stress. One item on the test was as follows: There are a number of pieces of toy fruit, including a large and a small strawberry. The experimenter says "Bert doesn't want to eat the BIG strawberry. What do you think he wants to eat?" Children who understand the pragmatic device of contrastive stress will answer "the little one." Children who do not know about contrastive stress will select any piece of fruit. Each child received a contrastive stress score, based on his performance on the test. They were also tested for obedience to Principle B on sentences such as "Bert is hitting him" (read without contrastive stress, of course). They found that the children who appeared to disobey Principle B had low stress scores. Those who had high scores on the stress test, however, performed like adults on the Principle B sentences. This was exactly the result predicted by their theory.

There are a few remaining problems with this account, however. First, adults usually allow coreference despite contraindexing exclusively with first and second person pronouns. (After you have read this section, you will start noticing examples of this behavior in yourself and others.) Experiments always contain sentences with third person pronouns (for obvious reasons). We need to find out how the issue of the person of the pronoun interacts with the phenomenon of contrastive stress. Furthermore, we need to test McDaniel and Maxfield's assumption that all instances of adults' use of coreference despite contraindexing are accompanied by contrastive stress on the pronoun. (For instance, in the Brigitte Bardot sentence, *me* is not contrastively stressed, but perhaps that is why it becomes a joke.) These problems do not compromise McDaniel and Maxfield's theory; they only suggest that the contrastive stress hypothesis requires further investigation.

McDaniel and Maxfield (1992) are the only researchers who have actually identified a pragmatic device for signaling apparent Principle B violations and tested children's knowledge of that pragmatic device. Grodzinsky and Reinhart (1993), however, have suggested a different kind of pragmatic principle that might be operating to distinguish children from adults. They suggested the following rule: If a speaker has the intent to communicate coreference, and there is a grammatical device available that will unambiguously convey that information (i.e., the bound-coindexed reflexive), then the speaker will choose that grammatical device for his message. Even though coreference despite contraindexing does not violate any linguistic principle, it will not be used when a clearer grammatical device is available. According to this theory, if I hear someone say "Grover hit him," I'll think (unconsciously, of course), "Well, if he wanted to tell me that Grover hit Grover, he would have said 'Grover hit himself.' But he didn't. He said 'Grover hit him.' While that could mean (grammatically) that Grover hit Grover, if he had meant to communicate that message, he would have formulated it differently. So he must mean that Grover hit someone else." Note that this is not a pragmatic principle determining when adults can use coreference despite contraindexing (as are McDaniel & Maxfield's and Wexler & Chien's); it is, instead, a pragmatic principle that adults use when they are interpreting the meaning of sentences such as "Grover hit him." They unconsciously consider the various grammatical devices available to the speaker and figure out which would be the optimal one under the circumstances; they then make an inference about the meaning being conveyed based on whether the speaker used the optimal grammatical structure. (Notice that in neither of the examples above would the reflexive have conveyed an identical message; an adult speaker would realize this by comparing the two possible formulations.) Grodzinsky and Reinhart suggested that such an inferential chain might tax the short-term memory capacity of children, so they do not undertake it and, hence, produce apparent violations of Principle B. No one has tested Grodzinsky and Reinhart's proposal directly; it's difficult to know just how that would be possible. However, Waltzman (1994; Waltzman & Cairns, 1995) did find a small but significant correlation between obedience to Principle B and verbal short-term memory.

A different connection between pragmatics and Principle B violation has been suggested recently by Foster-Cohen (1994). In this important paper, she explained how the Theory of Relevance, developed by Sperber and Wilson (1986, 1987), can explain the behavior of children in some psycholinguistic experiments. In brief, she suggested that when children are tested on their knowledge of Principle B, researchers must be very careful that the pragmatics of the situation is not masking the syntactic knowledge being tested. Although children expect the experimental situation to be pragmatically appropriate and process information accordingly, much of the dialogue in a typical Principle B experiment actually violates quite seriously the relevancy expectations of normal conversation. For instance, a typical scenario is to introduce Big Bird and Ernie, then to present the sentence "Big Bird is touching him," while Big Bird is touching himself, and to ask whether the sentence is true. The child has been led to believe that Ernie will be relevant to the following utterance and is trying to disentangle the oddity of the pragmatic situation in which he finds himself; thus, he makes errors on the sentences of interest to the experimenter.

A particularly interesting experiment with respect to Principles A and B was conducted by McKee, Nicol, and McDaniel (1993). It is one of the few experiments investigating what happens when children are actually listening to sentences in real time. This is called *on-line processing* and is almost always what is studied in psycholinguistic studies of adult language processing. Studies with children, however, are usually *off-line* in the sense that the children are asked to point to pictures, manipulate toys, or give judgments after they have heard and processed a sentence. McKee et al. used an experimental paradigm that has been used often and successfully with adult subjects, known as the *cross-modal priming* task. It is designed to identify (among other things) reference assignments that are made during sentence processing. In the McKee et al. study there were sentences such as "The alligator knows that the leopard is patting (himself or him) on the head with a soft pillow." At the moment the child (who was listening with headphones) heard either *himself* or *him*, he was shown (on a screen) a picture of a leopard and had to push either a "yes" or a "no" button indicating whether the picture is of a living thing. (Of course, all the responses to the experimental sentences were "yes"; there were other sentences during which pictures of inanimate objects were shown.) The idea of the cross-modal priming task is that if the noun (*the leopard*) is taken as coreferential with the pronoun (*himself* or *him*), the word *leopard* will be reactivated in the child's mind and he will respond to the picture faster than he would if the picture of the leopard appears after *the nurse* in the sentence, "The alligator knows that the leopard is patting the nurse on the head with a soft pillow." All the children, who ranged in age from 4 years, 1 month, to 6 years, 4 months (and all the adults), showed very fast responses following the reflexive *himself*, indicating that they were applying Principle A immediately when the reflexive was initially processed. The adults showed no reactivation of *leopard* following *him*, however, indicating that they were obeying Principle B on-line. The children were a different story, however. McKee et al. gave them a judgment task and found that, whereas all 17 subjects obeyed Principle A consistently, only 10 of them consistently obeyed Principle B. The 10 children who obeyed Principle B in the judgment task performed like the adults in the on-line task, showing no reactivation of *leopard* following *him*. The 7 children who disobeyed Principle B in the judgment task, however, reactivated *leopard* in response to *him* as well as to *himself*. It appeared, then, that those children were disobeying Principle B during on-line sentence processing.

Although the Principle B puzzle remains unsolved and probably will for some time, it has two particularly interesting features. First, it is a nonadult characteristic of child language that persists in many children for a very long time. It may not be characteristic of all children learning English, but certainly of the majority. Also, children learning Italian and Spanish, languages in which there is a short form of pronouns that can be attached to the verb (know as a *clitic*) (McKee, 1992), do not show this long nonadult behavior with respect to Principle B. Second, it is an example of children's behavior being more determined by grammar, whereas adults' is more determined by pragmatics. If current accounts are on the right track, together they provide a convincing demonstration of a situation in which the child's knowledge of grammar is far ahead of his knowledge of pragmatics.

Of all the binding principles, Principle C has been investigated over the longest period of time. This is because the fact that a pronoun cannot c-command its referent was noticed very early in the history of contemporary linguistics (although the explanation was not always characterized in this way) (Reinhart, 1976; Ross, 1967). This grammatical requirement for noncoreference was investigated in both adult and child language long before it became incorporated into the Binding Theory as an entailment of Principle C. The first to investigate its acquisition was probably C. Chomsky (1969). With two exceptions, all the children in her study over the age of 6 knew that *he* could not refer to *Pluto* in "He knew that Pluto was sad," whereas 77% of her 5-year-olds allowed coreference between *he* and *Pluto*, in violation of Principle C.

More recent studies have reported variable ages at which children demonstrate knowledge of Principle C. Crain and McKee (1985), for instance, found that 79% of the 3-year-olds and 88% of the 4-year-olds in their study obeyed the principle and rejected ungrammatical coreference in sentences such as "He washed Luke Skywalker" and "He ate the hamburger when the Smurf was in the fence." More compatible with C. Chomsky's data than with Crain and McKee's was a study by Ingram and Shaw (1981) of children between the ages of 3 and 8. The authors reported that only 34% of their 5-year-olds obeyed Principle C by rejecting coreference in sentences such as "He is sad that Mickey is crying" and "He cried when Mickey got lost." It is not clear what aspects of these studies produced the variability in the data, but all agree that Principle C is mastered by the age of 6, if not earlier. This suggests that, in general, children obey Principle C earlier than they do Principle B.

The study by McDaniel et al. (1990) compared performance on all three of the binding principles in 20 children between the ages of 3 years, 9 months, and 5 years, 4 months. Only two of the youngest children disobeyed Principle C. Seven children (including those two) disobeyed Principle B. These seven included children of all ages. In the Waltzman (1994; Waltzman & Cairns, 1995) study of 63 third graders, there were significantly more B violations than C violations. The reason it is important to compare Principles B and C is because both involve restricted reference of personal pronouns. According to the Lexical Learning Hypothesis, once a child distinguishes reflexive pronouns from personal pronouns in his lexicon, the binding principles should become operative in his grammar. If pragmatic principles are responsible for the fact that the child's performance on Principle B sentences is different from that of the adult, then it would seem reasonable for the same principles to apply to the Principle C sentences, as well. The fact that they are responded to differently suggests that we need, in addition to an explanation for the delay of Principle B, an explanation for the difference between B and C.

A great deal of research has been done on children's interpretation of pronoun reference beyond that of direct relevance to the binding principles. In particular, it has been observed that children prefer forward coreference, as in "Grover said that he was tired," to backward coreference, as in "When he was tired, Grover went to bed" (with *Grover = he* in both cases). Because of the structure of the second sentence, *he* does not c-command *Grover*, so coreference is not ruled out by Principle C. The issue seems to be directionality. I delay discussion of this research until after the following section on Principles of Control. Before returning to the directionality issue, I need to discuss another phenomenon regarding children's interpretation of pronouns, which is related to control.

Principles of Control

The linguistic principle of control relates to the interpretation of yet another kind of pronominal element, one that is necessary for sentence interpretation, but is not spoken or written; it is PRO, called "Big Pro." Every sentence must have a subject, either spoken or silent. In languages such as Italian and Spanish, which we described as allowing subjectless sentences, the silent subjects are *pro* ("little pro"), a pronominal element that we don't have in English. In English we do have instances, however, of clauses in which a verb's subject is silent and represented by PRO. In particular, this occurs when the verb is not inflected for tense, as in "Grover told Bert PRO to jump over the fence" or "Grover hugged Bert before PRO jumping over the fence." Adult English speakers know that in the first sentence it is Bert (the object) who will jump over the fence, but in the second it is Grover, the subject. In such sentences we know the identity of the missing subject because we know which of the noun phrases in the sentence *controls* PRO. PRO and its controller are coindexed, so they must corefer. The Control Principle (which applies in all languages and is part of Universal Grammar) refers to the principle of c-command, as do the Binding Principles. It is the following: The controller of PRO is the closest c-commanding NP, if there is one. Otherwise, control is arbitrary.

Now we are in a position to understand why the first sentence above is object controlled, whereas the second is subject controlled. Figure 4.14 is a diagram of the first sentence. The embedded clause (with the PRO subject) is the complement of the verb phrase because it is closely related to the verb *tell*. Literally, "PRO to jump over the fence" is what was told, so it functions like a direct object of the verb. Because of the structure, both *Grover* and *Bert* c-command PRO (the first branching node above both of them is the uppermost S, which dominates PRO); however, it is the closest that is the controller, so Bert and PRO are coindexed and corefer. Thus, Bert is interpreted as the subject of *jump*.

The situation is different in the second sentence. The embedded clause is not closely related to the verb. In fact, it is an adverbial clause that tells when Grover hugged Bert. In Figure 4.15 this different relationship is captured by showing that the embedded clause is attached, not to the VP, as a complement, but to the uppermost S. It is called an

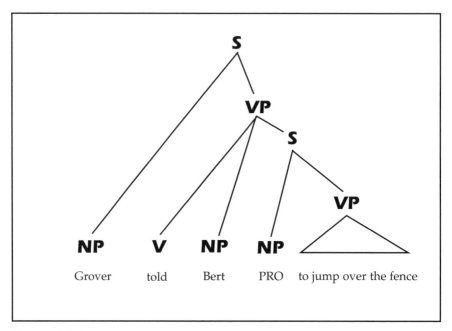

Figure 4.14

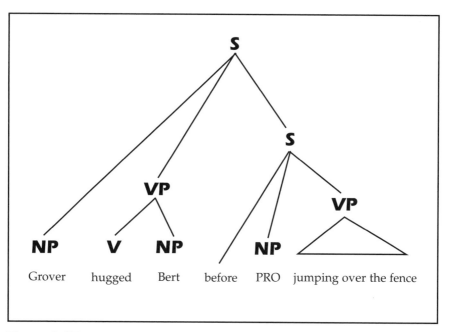

Figure 4.15

adjunct in this case. There are a variety of differences between adjunct and complement clauses. For instance, an adjunct clause can be preposed, to create "Before jumping over the fence, Grover hugged Bert." This cannot be done, however, with complements. "*To jump over the fence Grover told Bert" is not a well-formed sentence.

A consequence of the fact that the embedded clause is an adjunct is that only the subject of the matrix clause c-commands PRO. The object NP does not because the branching node immediately above it (VP) does not dominate PRO. Thus, the subject is the closest c-commanding NP; PRO is subject controlled, and the subject of the main clause is understood to be the subject of the tenseless verb *jumping*. Finally, the control rule mentions instances in which control of PRO is arbitrary, allowing it to refer outside the sentence. This is when there is no commanding NP. Thus, in a sentence such as "PRO filling out income tax returns is a pain," there is no c-commanding NP, so PRO can refer to any person who hates to fill out income tax forms.

C. Chomsky did the first study of the interpretation of sentences with infinitival complements in her study published in 1969. She found that children as young as 5 (her study investigated only children from 5 to 10) perform perfectly on sentences such as "Donald tells Mickey to jump up and down." Immature responses were associated with *promise* and *ask*, as discussed in Chapter 5 on lexical learning. Chomsky did not investigate adverbial adjuncts.

Tavakolian (1981) also investigated children's interpretation of infinitival complements (in the same study, mentioned above, that addressed relative clauses). She discovered that, unlike adults, some children allowed the subject of the matrix clause to serve as the subject of the infinitival verb. Thus, the example sentence "Grover told Bert to jump over the fence" would be interpreted as Grover telling Bert that he (Grover) was going to jump over the fence. Tavakolian extended her coordinated structure analysis to these sentences, suggesting that the embedded infinitive was not analyzed as a complement of the VP, but was, instead, coordinated with the matrix clause.

The first person to study children's interpretation of adverbial clauses with PRO subjects was Goodluck (1981). In a study of children 4 to 6 years of age, she discovered that many of the children enacted such sentences with the object performing the clausal action (unlike the adult interpretation). She proposed that such children were misanalyzing the embedded clause as a complement of the VP (as though it were an infinitival complement), resulting in a structure like the one shown in Figure 4.16. Application of the control rule to such a structure results in the object controlling PRO, since it is the closest c-commanding NP. Whereas Goodluck had reported only group data from her study, Hsu (1981; Hsu, Cairns, Eisenberg, & Schlisselberg, 1989; Hsu, Cairns, & Fiengo, 1985) analyzed the responses of individual children and demonstrated that some of them consistently act out such sentences with the object performing the clausal action; some consistently act it out with the subject (as an adult would); and others exhibited mixed responses, sometimes using the subject and sometimes the object.

McDaniel, Cairns, and Hsu (1990; 1990/1991) used an interview technique they had developed (McDaniel & Cairns, 1990, in press) that enabled them to discover all the interpretations a child might have of a particular sentence. This technique has a distinct advantage over the act-out task, because the child is likely to enact only the preferred in-

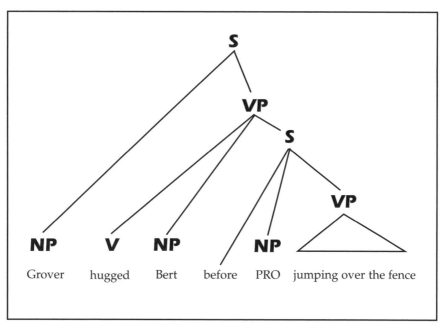

Figure 4.16

terpretation of a sentence, even if others are available. Using this technique, McDaniel et al. discovered that some children will allow either Grover, Bert, or Ernie (who is not mentioned in the sentence) to jump over the fence in the sentence "Grover hugged Bert before jumping over the fence." They explain this interpretation as expanding Tavakolian's coordinated clause analysis; Figure 4.17 illustrates the coordinate clause analysis of adverbial sentences. In such a structure, there is no c-commanding NP for PRO; hence, its control is arbitrary. This means that PRO can refer to anyone, inside or outside the sentence.

McDaniel et al.'s (1990/1991) study included infinitival sentences as well as adverbials. They determined that each of the children, aged 3 years, 9 months, to 5 years, 4 months, could be classified as having one of the following grammar types (GTs):

- *GT IA:* Children with this grammar type are coordinating both adverbial and infinitival sentences. They say that

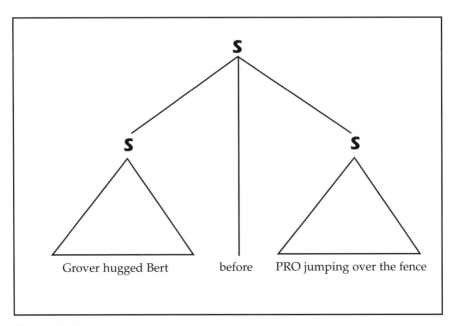

Figure 4.17

anyone in or out of the sentence can be performing the clausal action in both types of sentences.

- *GT IB:* These children have acquired the correct analysis for the infinitival sentences (e.g., Figure 4.14), so they interpret such sentences, as do adults, as being object controlled. However, they are still coordinating the adverbials, so will still allow anyone to perform the clausal action in adverbials.

- *GT II:* These children have object control in the infinitives but also in the adverbials. They consistently analyze the adverbial as a complement of the VP (as in Figure 4.16, which is unlike the adult structural analysis).

- *GT III:* These children have object control consistently in the infinitives, but for the adverbials, they sometimes allow object control, other times subject control. This is a transitional stage, in which the children sometimes analyze the adverbial as a complement of the VP and sometimes as an adjunct, attached to the uppermost S node. Crucially, however, the children never allow PRO to refer to someone outside the sentence.

- *GT IV:* These children have completely adult grammars with respect to control. The infinitives are object controlled; the adverbials are consistently subject controlled (S attached).

McDaniel et al. (following Hsu et al., 1985) proposed that these grammar types constitute a developmental sequence. They did not claim that every child would necessarily go through all the grammar types in the course of development. However, everyone would begin with GT I and end with GT IV. A longitudinal study reported in McDaniel et al. (1990/1991) and another reported by Cairns, McDaniel, Hsu, and Rapp (1994) confirmed this developmental sequence. Children often skip GT II, moving directly from GT I (often skipping GT IB) to GT III. A few children move directly from GT I to GT IV. In neither of these studies did children regress from a grammar type that required control (II, III, or IV) to one that allowed arbitrary control (IA or IB).

Whereas acquisitionists want to describe the child's developing grammar, we also want to account for changes in grammars. Our accounts are constrained, however, in that we must show that the child's evolving grammar is compatible with UG (Pinker's, 1984, Continuity Theory), and the mechanisms for change rely only on lexical learning (Wexler & Chien's, 1985, Lexical Learning Theory) and positive evidence (Learnability Theory). McDaniel et al. (1990/1991) account for grammatical development with respect to control completely through lexical learning. When the child learns that verbs such as *tell* take clausal complements, he will abandon his coordinate analysis and begin to embed the infinitival clauses into the VP, as does the adult, resulting in object control of PRO. Similarly, when he discovers that conjunctions such as *before* are subordinating rather that coordinating conjunctions, he will begin to embed the adverbials, sometimes attaching them to the VP, sometimes to the uppermost S. Once he thoroughly understands the adverbial nature of these clauses, he will consistently attach them to the uppermost S. Thus, grammatical development is really driven by lexical learning. This is a point to which I return in the next chapter.

The Pronoun Coreference Requirement

In the course of investigating control in sentences with embedded adverbial clauses, McDaniel et al. (1990/1991) discovered a curious phenomenon regarding many of the children's interpretation of pronouns. In a sentence such as "Grover hugged Bert before he jumped over the fence" many children would identify the same referent for the pronoun as they had for the controller of PRO in the sentence "Grover hugged Bert before jumping over the fence." They were not the first researchers to observe a similar patterning between PRO and real pronouns. Tavakolian (1978), Lust, Solan, Flynn, Cross, and Schuetz (1986), and Goodluck (1987) all reported such findings with group data. Hsu et al. (1985) analyzed individual children's act-out responses and found the same similarity.

For adults, pronouns in such constructions are free to refer either inside or outside the sentence. In fact, as mentioned earlier, in English there are no rules or principles that require a pronoun (other than a reflexive) to refer to a particular noun phrase in a sentence or to a particular character outside a sentence. Adults do, however, frequently have very strong preferences. In a sentence such as "John said that he was tired," for instance, most adults will prefer for *he* to refer to *John*. If, however, they are invited to imagine a scene in which Pete has returned from heavy exercise, they will realize that the pronoun can, of course, also refer to Pete. When Lust et al. (1986) and Hsu et al. (1985) first reported their results, everyone assumed that they were identifying strong preferences in the children, analogous to the preferences of adults.

When McDaniel et al. (1990/1991) developed their interview technique, it was possible to ask children whether a nonpreferred meaning was a possible interpretation. They presented children with sentences such as "Grover hugged Bert before he jumped over the fence" and provided a scenario in which Grover hugged Bert, and then Ernie (who was present in the scene) jumped over the fence. Everyone expected the children, like the adults, to accept a referent outside the sentence for the pronoun when the appropriate situational context was provided. To the experimenters' surprise, however, many of the children refused to allow an external referent for the pronoun, just as they refused to allow an external referent for PRO. McDaniel et al. labeled this the "pronoun coreference requirement" (PCR). The PCR was particularly interesting because it seemed to be related to control. No child with GT I (the grammar type in which PRO is allowed to refer outside the sentence) had the PCR. Furthermore, most of the time children with the PCR insisted that the pronoun refer to the same NP that controlled PRO in an adverbial sentence such as "Grover hugged Bert before jumping over the fence." It appeared, then, that the children were behaving as though the pronoun was controlled, although this is never the case in English.

In a longitudinal study of control and the PCR, Cairns, McDaniel, Hsu, and Rapp (1994) identified 9 of 14 children who had the PCR at some time during the course of the 9-month study. Those who demonstrated PCR ranged in age from 4 years, 4 months, to 5 years, 8 months, involving both the youngest and the oldest child in the study. For most of the children, the PCR extended beyond adverbial sentences to other kinds of complex sentences, such as "Grover told Bert that he was gonna jump over the fence." It does not hold for simple sentences, however. Children always allow an outside referent for simple sentences such as "Grover hugged him." (Even if they disobey Principle B by allowing *him* to refer to *Grover* in such sentences, they always allow an external referent, as well.)

The question arose, of course, as to whether the PCR is a feature of the grammar of many children, different from that of adult English speakers, or whether it is a pragmatic phenomenon, reflecting a stronger preference for internal reference than adults have. Cairns, McDaniel, Hsu, Parsons, and Konstantyn (1994; Cairns, McDaniel, Hsu, DeFino, & Konstantyn, in press) designed an experiment to resolve this question. They constructed a set of sentences such as "The pig hugged the sheep before she jumped rope" and gave them to children to determine whether they had the PCR. They used a slightly different version of the judgment task developed by McDaniel et al. (1990/1991). Instead of acting out the sentences and asking if the sentence was the "right way to say what happened," the researchers presented the child with three pictures (one at a time), depicting the clausal action being performed by the subject (Grover), the object (Bert), or a character not mentioned in the sentence (Ernie). The child was asked to select which picture or pictures matched the events described in the sentence. Of 44 children, 25 demonstrated the PCR. On another day, sentences of the same type were given to the same children, but this time they were preceded by a short story that biased the interpretation of the pronominal element to the character not mentioned in the sentence. Cairns, McDaniel, Hsu, Parsons, and Konstantyn (1994) assumed that if the PCR is a pragmatic phenomenon, the biasing context would cause the children to select an external referent for the pronoun. If, on the other hand, it is a grammatical phenomenon, there would be no more external referents selected than for PRO, the control of which is certainly a grammatical phenomenon. A group of adults were also run as subjects in the experiment.

The results were very clear. The children who were identified on the first day as having the PCR did not select external referents for the pronouns the following day, even with a story biasing their responses. Adults showed a preference for internal referents, but did select external referents whether or not the sentences followed the biasing story. It appears, then, that children with the PCR have a grammatical characteristic that adults do not have. Adults have a preference for internal reference between a pronoun in a complex sentence and another NP in the other clause; however, for some children such coreference is not simply a preference, but a requirement that is not altered by biasing context. There are some very interesting features of the PCR, which is as yet very poorly understood. One is that it is yet another instance in which children seem to be less susceptible to pragmatic effects and more controlled by a grammatical phenomenon than adults are. Another is that the PCR represents a learnability paradox. The children have developed such a grammar despite the fact that they must hear pronouns in complex sentences with external referents many times every day. What positive evidence, then, could cause them to eliminate the PCR from their grammars?

The PCR is not a rare phenomenon; many children have been shown to have it. Neither is it at all clear at what age it disappears from the child population. In all the studies cited, the oldest children are among those with the PCR. In many ways, the PCR makes us think of the widespread disobedience to Binding Principle B. Both are nonadult responses to personal pronouns, and both continue into late childhood. However, there is no obvious relationship between them. Cairns, McDaniel, Hsu, Parsons, and Konstantyn (1994) found that about half of the PCR children violated Principle B and another half did not. A great deal needs to be learned about both of these pronominal phenomena in either the referential systems or the grammatical systems of young children.

Other Studies of Pronominal Reference

We are now in a position to return to an issue raised above—the finding by many researchers that young children avoid backward coreference. Forward coreference refers to the situation when a noun phrase precedes its pronominal referent, as in "Bert jumped up and down when he found the penny" (where *Bert* = *he*). Backward coreference occurs when the pronoun precedes its referent, as in "When he found the penny, Bert jumped up and down." A number of issues come together in the investigation of coreference in complex sentences.

First, there is the existence of Principle C, or for our purposes, the universal principle stating that a pronoun cannot c–command its referent. This constraint does not apply to the backward coreference case in the paragraph above. Because of the structure of the sentence (both clauses are attached to a higher S node), *he* does not c-command *Bert* in that sentence. It would, however, rule out coreference between *him* and *deer* in the sentence "The zebra tells him that the deer will jump over the fence." This is because the clause "that the deer will jump over the fence" is a complement of the verb *tell*, so *him* c-commands *the deer*. Thus, there are some cases of backward coreference that are ruled out by grammatical principles (when the pronoun that precedes a potential referent c-commands it) and some that are not.

Another issue to consider is the pronoun coreference requirement, which is the requirement (for many children roughly aged 4 and over) that if a pronoun occurs in a complex sentence, it must find its referent in the other clause of the sentence. Cairns, McDaniel, Hsu, and Rapp (1994) demonstrated that children with the PCR extend it to preposed adverbial clauses, such as "Before he jumped over the fence, Bert hugged Ernie," as well as nonpreposed adverbials, which were studied initially. Children with the PCR, therefore, require backward coreference in sentences such as "When he found the penny, Bert jumped up and down."

Finally, there is the directionality issue. A large number of researchers over the years have found that young children avoid backward coreference. For example, Lust (1981) reported that in an elicited imitation task children manifested more errors on backward sentences such as "After he jumped over the fence, the deer ate the grass" than on forward sentences such as "The deer ate the grass after he jumped over the fence." Additional researchers using a variety of tasks (Chomsky, 1969; Ingram & Shaw, 1981; Lust & Clifford, 1986; Solan, 1983; Tavakolian, 1978) have reported that some children manifest consistent patterns of external reference (i.e., selecting a character not mentioned in the sentence as the antecedent of the pronoun) both in cases where backward coreference is ruled out by Principle C and in cases where it is not. Most of these researchers agreed that children had a nonadult grammatical rule prohibiting backward coreference. Crain and McKee (1985) and Goodluck (1987), however, demonstrated that children will allow backward coreference, supporting the position that the findings with respect to backward coreference are a processing (performance) phenomenon, rather than a grammatical one. Although Ingram and Shaw (1981) reported that many of their subjects avoided backward coreference, they also found that some of their younger children manifested a pattern of internal coreference in both kinds of backward cases (violating Principle C in those cases where the pronoun c-commanded its referent).

Hsu, Cairns, Eisenberg, and Schlisselberg (1991) designed a study to compare all these factors simultaneously across a wide age range, 3 to 8 years, as well as a group of adults. Among the sentences they gave the subjects in an act-out task were the following:

- Backward coreference disallowed by Principle C:
  The zebra tells him that the deer will jump over the fence.

- Backward coreference not disallowed by Principle C:
  The zebra touches him after the deer jumps over the fence.

- Forward coreference:
  The zebra touches the deer after he jumps over the fence.

An animal not mentioned in the sentence was included along with a zebra and a deer in the array of toys available for act-out; it was clear to the subjects that they could use all three of the toys if they chose to do so. The researchers found that with respect to the backward coreference sentences, there were three identifiable response patterns. The first, used by the younger children (average age 4 years, 10 months) was a pattern of internal coreference, even in the cases disallowed by Principle C. Hsu et al. suggested that in these cases the PCR comes in conflict with Principle C. Although the fact that the pronoun c-commands the noun phrase in the embedded sentence should prohibit coreference, the PCR demands that there be coreference within the embedded clause. Thus, a child may allow coreference not because he does not know the constraint imposed by Principle C, but because the PCR is a stronger determinant of sentence interpretation. (Cairns, McDaniel, Hsu, & Rapp, 1994, reported a similar analysis.) Older children (average age 6 years, 1 month) demonstrated the familiar pattern of avoiding backward coreference in both cases, but this was the least common of the three patterns. Adults and the oldest children (average age 6 years, 3 months) exhibited a pattern in which they avoided coreference disallowed by Principle C, but allowed it in the cases where the pronoun did not c-command its referent.

It appears, then, that children do not begin with a prohibition against backward coreference, either in their grammars or in their performance systems. Neither do we know whether it is a phenomenon associated with all children. In any event, it is almost certainly not a feature of child grammar. The children in the Cairns, McDaniel, Hsu, and Rapp (1994) study who did not have the PCR said that it was possible for the pronoun to refer to either Grover, Bert, or an external character in sentences with preposed adverbial clauses such as "Before he jumped over the fence, Grover hugged Bert." Recall that their study used an interview technique, so it was possible to identify all possible interpretations of the sentences, not merely the preferred one. It is certainly the case, however, that English-speaking adults and children prefer forward to backward coreference (possibly because English is a right-branching language). Beliavsky (1994) collected narratives from 57 children from kindergartners to third graders and also from a group of 5 adults. Virtually all the pronouns used by all her subjects were in constructions indicating forward coreference. Almost never did either a child or an adult construct a piece of narrative in which the pronoun preceded its referent. We seem to have a discourse requirement (a performance characteristic, not part of the grammar) that the subject of a pronoun should be available in the discourse context before it is used in a sentence. I have a bit more to say about the use of pronouns in narratives in the final chapter.

CHAPTER 5

Lexical Learning

It has been estimated that the 6-year-old child has a vocabulary of from 8,000 to 14,000 words (Carey, 1978). Beginning with 1 word at 12 months, this means that the child must acquire an average of 4 to 8 new words every day during the preschool years. The lexical acquisition process begins gradually, with early lexical items often being quite deliberately taught by the child's caretakers. Around the age of 18 months, however, lexical acquisition speeds up and new words are learned very rapidly, with less and less explicit instruction. Psycholinguists call this the vocabulary "spurt" or "explosion" (Dromi, 1987).

Bates and her colleagues have reported the results of a massive project to assess early lexical and grammatical development using a parental report instrument, the *MacArthur Communicative Development Inventories* (Bates et al., 1994; Marchman & Bates, 1994). In this 10-year study, they have gathered data from 1,803 infants and toddlers in the early stages of language acquisition. Findings indicate a gradual increase in vocabulary size, with a median of 6 words at 1 year of age; 44 at 1 year, 4 months; 170 at 1 year, 8 months; 311 at 2 years; and 574 at 2 years, 6 months. At each age period, however, there is enormous individual variation. For example, at 2 years, the top 10% of their sample had vocabularies over 534 words, whereas the bottom 10% had fewer than 57 words. An analysis of the composition of the children's vocabularies in terms of word type showed that common nouns always predominate, but begin a proportional decrease when vocabulary size reaches about 100 words. At this time there is a steady increase in the proportion of verbs and other predicates, with the greatest gains taking place between 100 and 400 words. Closed class (function) words remain proportionally very low and constant until vocabulary size reaches 400 words; there is then a sharp proportional increase in the incidence of closed class words (Bates et al., 1994). The researchers suggest that these data point to three "waves" of lexical organization: from reference to predication to grammar.

Lexical acquisition is remarkable not only because of its speed, but because of the amount of information that the child must encode about each lexical item. Every word has associated with it not only a phonological representation and a particular meaning, but also information regarding the structures in which it can participate. This is most obvious in the case of verbs. *Hit* must have a direct object; *sleep* must not; and an object is optional for verbs such as *read*. The verb *tell* allows a clausal complement to appear in its verb phrase: "Bert told Grover to jump up and down." However, while a verb such as *kissed* does not: "*Bert kissed Grover to jump up and down" is not possible (unless, of course, we mean that Bert kissed Grover in order to jump up and down, in which case the clause is an adjunct, rather than a complement of the verb). *Grammatical* relations of a verb are called its *arguments*. Thus, a verb such as *sleep* has only one argument, its subject; *hit* has two, its subject and its object. Some verbs have three arguments, such as *give*, which requires a subject, a direct object, and an indirect object.

Nouns also have structural requirements associated with them. Thus, mass nouns, such as *rice* or *water* differ from count nouns, such as *dog*, in that they do not take plural markers (*rices*), they cannot be preceded by the indefinite article (*a rice*) or by plural demonstratives (*these rice*) and they cannot be modified by the cardinal numbers (*three rice*). Proper nouns are not preceded by articles, but common nouns are.

Nouns, verbs, and adjectives are content words. They are also known as *open class* words because new words of these types can always be added to the lexicon of a language. Function words are also known as *closed class* because new words of these types cannot be added to the lexicon. There cannot be any new prepositions, articles, or conjunctions in English, whereas new nouns appear daily. Function words obviously play syntactic roles. Conjunctions can be either coordinating or subordinating, so they control the structural relationship between the clauses they connect. Articles introduce phrases; complementizers and relative pronouns introduce clauses; and so on. Clearly, then, when a child acquires a lexicon, she acquires far more than a set of meanings for lexical items; she must also acquire the structural information connected with each word. There is often a clear relationship between the meaning of a word and the structures associated with it. *Tell* clearly takes both a direct object and a clausal complement because to *tell*, one must tell someone something. The intimate relationship between meaning and structure can assist the word-learning child in two ways: Knowing details of a word's meaning can lead the child to acquire its syntactic properties, and observing how a new word behaves syntactically can provide clues to its meaning.

Lexical learning is essential to a theory of syntactic development, as described in the preceding chapter. Unfortunately, however, we do not have a neat theory of word learning as we do of the acquisition of grammar. Because words are language specific, their acquisition is probably even more dependent on information from the speech of the environment than is the case with syntax. It appears that information about words is more available to the child than is information about syntax. In a sense this is true. Very early words are explicitly taught, and children are always able to ask adults the meanings of words. However, as in syntax, a great deal of learning goes on without explicit instruction. After the vocabulary spurt begins at the end of the child's second year of life, a great deal of rapid word learning takes place in the absence of explicit instruction; in fact, children probably learn many words in the absence of personal experience by observing others use them. Carey (1978) conducted a study in which she taught 3- and 4-year-olds a new color name, simply by mentioning it in their nursery school. It was instantly classified by the children as a color word, a process Carey called "fast mapping," but the details of its meaning and its relationship to the other color words the children knew were worked out more slowly over time. Although negative evidence is theoretically possible with respect to lexical learning, it is probably not much of a factor; children receive little systematic correction of lexical errors and must rely principally on positive evidence, as in the acquisition of grammar.

Actually, very little is known about the mechanisms by which children acquire such an impressive lexicon in such a brief period of time. It is, however, an activity of all language-learning children, so whatever the mechanisms are, we can assume that they are part of the biologically based language-learning faculty of humans. Initially, lexical learning seems to be very different from acquisition of grammar. On closer inspection, however, they seem quite similar at a theoretical level. Both are the result of the interaction of biologically based, language-particular acquisition mechanisms with the speech of the environment. Like acquisition of syntax, acquisition of the lexicon occurs with insufficient specific teaching to account for the rapidity and accuracy with which it is learned; also, both rely primarily on positive evidence.

Learning Words for Objects

All languages have words, in the grammatical category *noun*, that map onto concrete objects. Object words are the earliest acquired and make up the largest proportion of any word type in children's early lexicons (Bates et al., 1994; Gentner, 1983). Thus, an understanding of how children acquire words for objects would seem to be the most basic requirement of a theory of lexical learning. Gleitman began an important article on the acquisition of meaning with the following quotation by John Locke, the 17th-century British philosopher, on the general topic of learning words for objects: "If we observe how children learn languages, we will find that, to make them understand what the names of simple ideas or substances stand for, people ordinarily show them the thing whereof they would have them have the idea; and then repeat to them the name that stands for it, as 'white,' 'sweet,' 'milk,' 'sugar,' 'cat,' 'dog'" (Locke, 1690/1964, Book 3.IX.9; cited in Gleitman, 1990).

Locke's characterization of word learning is quite close to one that most people accept uncritically even today. We assume that the child observes a scene, an adult describes the scene, and the child then learns the words that the adult uses. However, as Gleitman pointed out with characteristic wit and wisdom, this cannot possibly be the way it works. Think of the simplest possible case. A dog is in view, say, lying on a couch. The adult points to the dog and says to the infant,

"See the doggie." How can the child know what the adult is referring to? It could be the couch-with-a-dog-lying-on-it, or it could be some part of the dog—its ear or tail. It is not at all clear how the child determines the exact extent of a word's referent even in such a simple situation. Another problem with the simple referential account arises when the adult and the child are not attending to the same object and the adult labels the one she is attending to. Suppose the child is looking out the window at a cat and the caretaker, looking at the dog on the couch, says, "That's a dog." Called *discrepant labeling*, this state of affairs (which is common) should be very disruptive to the child. Because, after the vocabulary spurt, children acquire words (at least an initial representation) after only one or two experiences of word–object mapping, discrepant labeling could result in many errors for a child who expects adults to provide names for the things she is attending to (as Locke's description would suggest). It is observations such as these that make inescapable the conclusion that children must bring some specialized learning mechanisms to the task of lexical acquisition.

In an important theoretical article, Golinkoff, Mervis, and Hirsh-Pasek (1994) suggested that there are some principles of lexical learning that guide early learning, which is characterized by slow acquisition and a great deal of caretaker input, and others that guide the later, rapid, spontaneous learning characteristic of the vocabulary spurt. Most basic is the *principle of reference*: that words refer to (or map to) objects, actions, and attributes in the environment. The earliest word use is usually referential, together with nonverbal pointing that the child clearly understands as referential. Infants enjoy naming things and often ask what objects are called. If, however, reference were simply associative, discrepant naming would produce many incorrect mappings. This, however, is not the case. Very young infants seem to possess enough awareness of the nonverbal behavior of the adults around them to protect them against incorrect mappings.

Baldwin (1991) studied the effects of *discrepant labeling* on a large group of infants between the ages of 16 and 19 months. In the *discrepant labeling* condition, two toys were presented to the child; she held one, while the other was placed in a container (e.g., a bucket). The experimenter waited until the child's attention was focused on the toy she was holding, then he looked into the bucket and named (with a novel word) the toy that he was looking at, but the child was not: "That's a peri." This procedure was repeated four times. In another condition the experimenter looked at and named the same toy that the child was looking at; Baldwin called this *follow-in labeling*. Of course, the children learned the novel labels for the visible toy in the follow-in labeling condition. What is fascinating about the study is that they did not make the incorrect mapping between the visible toy and the novel label in the discrepant labeling condition. Apparently, the children were able to observe that the experimenter's attention was not directed toward the same toy as theirs was, and this observation inhibited their mapping the novel label to the visible toy. Baldwin concluded, "The findings provided clear support for an early appreciation of the linguistic significance of the speaker's nonverbal cues. . . . What is significant is that infants possess abilities which buffer them from making errors during discrepant labeling" (p. 146). Clearly, then, for very young children engaged in simple referential learning, the mechanisms are far more sophisticated than the simple associative processes identified by Locke.

The referential principle quite possibly accounts for a well-attested characteristic of early child language, known as *underextension*. This refers to a situation in which a child adopts a very narrow, situation-specific reference for a new word. A classic example was reported by Bloom (1970) regarding her daughter, Allison. When Allison was around 1 year old, she restricted the referent of the word *bird* to the mobile above her dressing table. Bloom (Bloom & Lahey, 1978) also gave an example of a child's first meaning of *flower* being restricted to yellow jonquils. Similar to underextension in that the referential domain of a word is taken to be too small is the phenomenon noted by Rosch (1978) that class inclusion first consists of only prototypical (the "best") exemplars of each. Thus, robins and canaries will be considered birds, but not ostriches, penguins, and turkeys. Rosch suggested that the domain of reference of each class is initially its prototypical exemplars and then extends to include less optimal exemplars of that class.

My favorite personal example of underextension is from my son when he was about 2 1/2 years old. He had been at nursery school and was now at home, playing on the floor while I graded students' papers. He said, "Mommy, will you be my friend?" I assured him that his mommy was his friend, and went on grading papers. After a few more requests, he became quite insistent. It turned out that he wanted me to sit on the floor with him and work a jigsaw puzzle. It turned out that an older girl had come up to him in nursery school, said "Stewart, will you be my friend?" and had proceeded to sit on the floor and work a jigsaw puzzle with him. That's what he thought *friend* meant. What's nice about this example is not only that it is an example of underextension, but it is also an example of the role of maternal input into lexical learning. I did not give Stewart negative evidence by telling him that he had the meaning of *friend* wrong; I just abandoned my papers, sat on the floor, and worked a jigsaw puzzle with him. As far as I know, he never received any explicit instruction from anyone regarding the meaning of the word *friend* (which is quite complex, when you think about it). Yet, a few years later, at the age of 4 (probably earlier), he was able to use the word in all its semantic richness. The mechanisms by which the child arrives at precise word meanings is mysterious and quite astonishing when you observe it going on in a child you interact with often.

Another very early lexical learning principle is the *whole object principle* (Carey, 1978; Markman, 1992; Mervis, 1987), which states that upon hearing a novel word, the child will assume that it maps to an entire object, not to only parts of it. This principle prevents the child from thinking that *rabbit* refers to a rabbit's tail or ear, but instead to the entire animal (a fundamental problem of induction pointed out by Quine, 1960). Support for this early principle comes from examining the child's early words. While object words are most common among the child's early words, there are typically very few for object parts (Mervis, 1990). There is also experimental evidence to support the existence of the principle. Taylor and Gelman (1988) demonstrated that 2-year-olds would construe a label for a novel object to be a label for the whole object and not for a salient attribute of the object (in that case a bright pattern). Mervis and Long (1987) also demonstrated that children 1 year, 6 months, to 2 years, 0 months, in age interpreted a label for a part of an object as the label for the whole object. A study by Golinkoff, Kenealy, and Hirsh-Pasek (1993; cited in Golinkoff et al., 1994) demonstrated that this principle is a feature of word mapping, rather than perceptual salience. If a novel word was used, the whole object principle was demonstrated. If there was no label, the object part was selected as an exemplar of the object about 25% of the time.

Another early lexical learning principle is the *principle of extendibility*, which is simply that one word can map onto other similar objects. This may be one of the factors producing the well-known feature of early word learning known as *overextension*, in which all entities sharing a particular perceptual feature are called by the same word. Most familiar are examples such as calling all men "Daddy" or all four-legged animals "doggie," but the literature is filled with more exotic examples involving the overextension of many different perceptual features, including taste (everything sweet is *candy*), movement (any moving animal is a *bird*), and texture (everything soft is a *kitty*) (Bloom & Lahey, 1978). Overextension seems to be universal, continuing until the child's vocabulary is well established soon after the age of 2. It hardly seems plausible to suppose that children actually fail to discriminate perceptually or to have different conceptual categories for, say, dogs and cats, yet why do they use the same word for both? Fremgen and Fay (1980), in a simple and elegant experiment, demonstrated that children who overextend in production do not overextend in receptive tasks. They obtained information from the mothers of children 1 year, 2 months, to 2 years, 2 months, of age regarding which lexical items their children overextended and to what referents. They then showed each child pictures of the overextended referents and asked them to point to the overextended word. Thus, if a child overextended *doggie* to cats, Fremgen and Fay would show her a picture of a dog and a cat and say "Show me the doggie." The child never pointed to the cat. Thus, it is not the case that the overextending child really believes cats are dogs, or fails to discriminate perceptually or conceptually between dogs and cats. It is simply that the child has a very limited productive vocabulary (one which, in this case, does not contain the word *cat*), so when she wants to talk about a cat, she simply selects the semantically closest available word (Bloom & Lahey, 1978; de Villiers & de Villiers, 1978; Fremgen & Fay, 1980). The conclusion is that, while the principle of extendibility enables overextension, it is the child's limited vocabulary that drives it. In fact, overextension is primarily a feature of very early lexical learning and no longer occurs after the vocabulary spurt (Nelson, 1988).

There is, however, a principle of later lexical learning that is related to extendibility, enabling the child to acquire words that refer to categories of things, while not overextending inaccurately. It is necessary for the child to acquire category labels, such as *dog* that refer to indefinitely many related animals, while not extending falsely to, say, cats. This principle is really in two parts, the simplest of which is probably operative in early learning (Golinkoff et al., 1994). Related to the whole object principle, it is that words map onto objects rather than properties of those objects, such as their motion. A study by Echols (1992; reported in Golinkoff et al., 1994) presented infants 9 months to 1 year, 2 months, of age with a novel word that could be construed as applying to either a novel object or a novel motion. They selected the object rather than the motion as the referent of the novel label.

The second part of the principle is that, when object names are extended, they will be extended to other objects of a category, as opposed to being extended to relationships between that object and another object. This general principle has been called the *taxonomic principle* by Markman and Hutchinson (1984; Markman, 1990); a very similar concept is *categorical scope*, proposed by Golinkoff et al. (1994). The idea here is that the word *dog* will be extended to other creatures in the category dog, rather than to any other thematically related property of dogs, such as running dogs or dogs who are eating bones. Markman and Hutchinson demonstrated this principle by showing that if given a label, 4- and 5-year-old children would identify a pig, but not milk, as being an exemplar of the same label as a cow, even though milk is thematically but not categorically related to cow. Without the label, the children chose the categorically related object only 25% of the time, demonstrating that this is a principle of word learning, rather than a result of perceptual salience.

A final principle of later lexical acquisition is that novel names will map to unnamed categories (Golinkoff et al., 1994), which is closely related to a principle articulated by Markman, called the *mutual exclusivity assumption*, by which children assume that each object has one and only one label. It is interesting to compare this principle to the categorizing principle; while an indefinite number of dogs can all share the category name *dog*, an individual dog can only be called a dog. This principle obviously has to be violated if the child is to learn that a particular dog can also be a pet, an animal, or Fido. In fact, according to Markman (1990), children find class inclusion difficult because it violates the mutual exclusivity assumption. It allows children to learn words for parts of things, however, despite the whole object principle. If a child has a name for an animal, say a rabbit, and hears the word *ear*, by the mutual exclusivity assumption she will not map *ear* as another word for rabbit. Instead, she will select a part of the rabbit for its referent. Of course, the mutual exclusivity assumption is a guiding principle; with sufficient contradictory information, the child can acquire class inclusion words (Markman, 1992). In a series of experiments Markman and Wachtel (1988) demonstrated that if children are presented with several objects, all but one of which has a known label, and a new label is provided, they will map it onto the unnamed object.

Closely related to the mutual exclusivity assumption is the principle that a language community will have one conventional word for referents and that is the only mapping that is correct. Originally articulated by Clark (1983), it is closely related to Pinker's (1991) uniqueness principle and is used to account for children's retreat from a number of immature forms. Very young children often adopt idiosyncratic terms for objects, then give them up in favor of more conventional labels. Mervis (cited in Golinkoff et al., 1994) reported that her son initially called pacifiers "pops," but later used the nursery word only in the presence of family members, adopting the conventional "pacifier" for nonfamily members. This demonstrates the gradual acquisition of a conventional term, which will eventually drive out the idiosyncratic form. Dromi (1987; reported by Golinkoff et al., 1994) noted that nonconventional, idiosyncratic forms predominated in her daughter's lexicon until she had a vocabulary of 150 words. Many children make errors of the type "to broom," but abandon them when they acquire the conventional "to sweep." The uniqueness principle has even been appealed to as an account of how children escape from overgeneralizations such as *eated* and *goed* in the absence of negative evidence. The presence of the conventional *ate* and *went* eventually pushes the unconventional derived forms from the child's lexicon.

Learning Words for Actions

Many problems the child encounters in identifying labels for objects also occur in identifying the referents for verbs. In fact, as Gleitman (1990) pointed out, the situation with even very simple verbs may be even worse: "Consider the learning of simple motion verbs, such as 'push' or 'move.' In a satisfying proportion of the times that caretakers say something like 'George pushes the truck,' George can be observed to be pushing the truck. But unless George is a hopeless incompetent, every time he pushes the truck, the truck will move. So a verb used by the caretaker to describe this event may represent one of these ideas ('push') or the other ('move')" (p. 14).

Gleitman's solution to some of these problems is what she calls *syntactic bootstrapping*. I mentioned in Chapter 4 Pinker's (1984) theory of semantic bootstrapping in which he proposed that the meaning of an event and the words used to describe it help the child "get into" simple sentence structure via linking rules. Syntactic bootstrapping occurs when the child uses the structure of a sentence to predict word meanings. Brown, of Adam, Eve, and Sarah fame, demonstrated this phenomenon many years ago (1957) in the following way. He showed 3- to 5-year-olds a picture of some spaghetti-like material being poured into a vessel. Some of the children were asked to show "some blick"; they pointed to the spaghetti. Others were asked to show "a blick"; they chose the vessel. The children who were asked to show "blicking" referred to the action being carried out. Clearly, the grammatical markers *some, a,* and *–ing* identified the mass noun, the count noun, and the verb, respectively. The children were using their knowledge of grammar to identify the referent of the nonsense word.

In a contemporary test of syntactic bootstrapping, Gleitman (1990) also constructed nonsense words, which she presented to children in sentential contexts while they were observing videotaped scenes. For example, some children would see a scene of a rabbit eating and hear the sentence, "The rabbit moaks." Others would see a scene of an elephant feeding a rabbit and hear, "The elephant moaks the rabbit." In posttesting it was revealed that the former children thought that *moaks* meant "eat" and the latter group thought that it meant "feeds." For the second group, *moaks* could have been ambiguous, just as *push* was in the sentence about George and the truck. It could have meant either that the elephant was doing something to the rabbit or that the rabbit was doing something independent of the elephant. It is only the fact that the children attended to the subject–verb–object structure of the sentence that they were able to correctly identify *moaks* as the former type of word, rather than the latter.

Further confirmation of the syntactic bootstrapping hypothesis comes from the work of Naigles (1990), who used a preferential looking experimental paradigm with 2-year-old children. In this paradigm, the child is seated on her mother's lap in front of a television screen and is introduced to a novel verb, such as *gorp*, while observing the following video scene of novel events: A rabbit and a duck (graduate students dressed in animal costumes) are interacting. The rabbit repeatedly pushes the duck down into a squatting position, and the duck pops back up each time. Meanwhile, they are both making big circles in the air with their arms. Thus, there is one novel transitive action going on (the pushing) and one novel intransitive action (the arm wheeling). Half the children hear a voice say the sentence, "The rabbit is gorping the duck" (a novel transitive verb) and the others hear "The rabbit and the duck are gorping" (a novel intransitive verb). Then the children are presented with two screens. On one the rabbit is pushing the duck (with no arm wheeling); on the other the rabbit and duck are wheeling their arms (with no pushing). The voice says "Where's gorping now? Find gorping!" Virtually every child in Naigles's study looked longer at the scene that matched the transitivity of the verb in the sentence the child heard in the training session.

Naigles's study is an impressive demonstration of the way syntax can guide young children's lexical development. All the children saw the same initial scene. *Gorping* could have referred to any aspect of the scene, but since it was used as a verb, all the children realized that it applied to an action. Two actions were being performed, however, and the children distinguished between them, as the referent of the novel verb, based on whether it had been used transitively or intransitively in the initial presentation. Thus, the syntactic evidence guides the child in her choice between two equally plausible semantic options.

Pinker (1991) identified a class of verbs, which he called "light" verbs, that have nonspecific meanings. Syntactically they are fullfledged verbs, but they are very versatile precisely because they have little internal semantic structure. These are verbs such as *come, go, make, be, bring, take, get,* and *give.* They often serve little more than a structural purpose in phrases such as "take a bath," "make love," and "go crazy." Children's early verb usage includes proportionately more light verbs than do their later lexicons. Jarmulowicz (1994) examined the transcript of one child from the age of 3 to 5 years and showed that 56% of her verb use was light verbs at the age of 3, but 46% at age 5. Watkins, Rice, and Moltz (1993) called them "general all-purpose verbs" and showed that 3- to 5-year-olds who were language impaired use more of this type of verb than do normally developing children.

It is not surprising that verbs with less restricted meanings are also understood better by young children than are verbs with very specific meanings, which are often misinterpreted in early acquisition. For example, *buy* and *sell* are initially interpreted as *take* and *give.* Another source of difficulty in the interpretation of verbs is those that shift meaning with respect to relation to speaker and hearer. For instance, terms involving direction of movement, such as *come–go* and *bring–take* present difficulties. As with other relational words, the child has difficulty using them when the perspective is not her own, with full contrasts not being achieved until early school age (Clark & Garnica, 1974).

C. Chomsky (1969) demonstrated lexical difficulty with highly related verbs. In her study, whose subjects were children between the ages of 5 and 10, she discovered that many children interpret *ask* as though it means *tell*. For this part of the study, she asked pairs of children to ask and tell each other various things. Here is an interchange between the experimenter and two of the children (p. 55), Christine (who is 5 years, 1 month, and is being instructed to ask and tell) and Eric Handel, her partner:

> EXPERIMENTER (to Christine): Ask Eric his last name.
>
> CHRISTINE: Handel.
>
> EXPERIMENTER: Ask Eric this doll's name.
>
> CHRISTINE: I don't know.
>
> EXPERIMENTER: Ask Eric what time it is.
>
> CHRISTINE: I don't know how to tell time.
>
> EXPERIMENTER: Tell Eric what class is in the library.
>
> CHRISTINE: Kindergarten.

The children made errors only when *ask* was being used to ask a question. When it was being used to make a request, they never confused its meaning with that of *tell*. An example is Eric (5 years, 2 months):

> EXPERIMENTER: Here are all the toys standing in line. Now suppose Mickey Mouse asks Bozo to go first. What does Mickey say?
>
> ERIC: Bozo, go first.

It is interesting to speculate how children who misinterpret *ask* might correct their lexical representation given only positive evidence. What is perhaps more surprising is the fact that they have such a misconception after more than 5 years of positive experience with such a high-frequency word.

Learning the Structural Properties of Verbs

In the previous chapter I reviewed the child's acquisition of principles of control. According to the theory proposed by McDaniel, Cairns, and Hsu (1990/1991) and Cairns, McDaniel, Hsu, and Rapp (1994), the change from Grammar Type (GT) IA to GT IB occurs when the child realizes that the clauses in an infinitival sentence such as "Grover told Bert PRO to jump over the fence" are not coordinated, but that the infinitival clause is embedded in (attached to) the verb phrase (see Figure 4.14). At that point, the universal principle of control identifies the object (in this case, Bert), the closest c-commanding NP, as the controller of PRO, and reference is no longer arbitrary (as it was in GT IA). This apparent dramatic reorganization of the child's grammar is effected (according to the theory described in Cairns et al., 1994) by acquisition of the lexical information that, for verbs such as *tell*, the clause stating what was told is an argument of the verb and therefore must be part of the verb phrase. This information about the structural characteristics of such verbs is intimately related to their meaning; to tell, one must tell something. This theory about the acquisition of control is a special case of the general proposition of the Continuity Theory of Pinker (1984) and the Lexical Learning Hypothesis of Wexler and Chien (1985) that grammatical development relies heavily on lexical learning. It is, therefore, of great importance to understand how children come to know the structural properties of verbs.

C. Chomsky (1969) was the first person to do an extensive study of children's understanding of verbs in infinitival complement constructions. Her subjects were children from 5 to 10 years of age. I have already discussed one aspect of her study, involving reference of pronouns in obedience to what is now known at Principle C of the Binding Theory. In another aspect of her study, she presented each child with Mickey Mouse and Donald Duck dolls. She said to the child, "Mickey tells Donald to jump up and down. Make him do it," and observed which doll the child made jump up and down. Thirty-six of the 40 children interpreted this kind of sentence in an adultlike manner, making Donald do the jumping. (Four exhibited some subject responses to this sentence; they are likely children whom we would now characterize as having arbitrary reference for PRO.) They performed very differently, however, on sentences with the verb *promise* than they did those with the verb *tell*. When the sentence was "Mickey promised Donald to jump up and down. Make him do it," many of the children, even the oldest ones, still made Donald do the jumping.

In 1969 when Chomsky's book was published, control was analyzed quite differently than it is now. The Minimal Distance Principle (Rosenbaum, 1965) was the ancestor of the current closest c-commanding NP and led to the object's being interpreted as the subject of the complement action with *tell*-type verbs (which we now think of as object control verbs). Chomsky's analysis was that *promise* is lexically marked as a verb that does not obey the Minimal Distance Principle; because it is an exception, information about it is acquired late.

The finding that children exhibit a nonadult interpretation of such sentences with *promise* is one of the most reliable findings in the child language literature (Eisenberg & Cairns, 1994; Sherman & Lust, 1992). We would now characterize it, rather than being an exception to the Minimal Distance Principle, as being an exception to the principle that the controller of PRO is the closest c-commanding NP, requiring it to be marked in the lexicon as a verb that requires subject control. In any event, Chomsky was the first to discover this pervasive error in children's knowledge of the syntactic properties of verbs.

In an extensive study of six different verb types, Eisenberg (1989; Eisenberg & Cairns, 1994) investigated what children aged 3 to 5 know about the control properties of verbs that can appear in infinitival constructions. The verbs she studied were the following:

1. *Tell* and *force*, which are the kinds of verbs I have discussed often in this book. These verbs must take a direct object and have a complement clause, the subject of which is PRO, as in "Bert told Grover PRO to leave."

2. *Ask* and *beg*, which can be used either with or without a direct object. If the object is present, the sentence is object controlled, as in "Grover asked Bert PRO to jump over the fence"; if not, it is subject controlled, as in "Grover asked PRO to jump over the fence."

3. *Want* and *like*, which can appear either with or without a direct object. These are special verbs because, while they

contain PRO as subject of the infinitive in sentences such as "Bert wants to go," there is no PRO in sentences such as "Bert wants Grover to go." This is because *Grover* is not the object of *want* as it is the object of *tell* in a sentence such as "Bert told Grover PRO to go." In that sentence Bert is telling Grover something (to go), but in "Bert wants Grover to go" it is not the case that Bert wants Grover; instead, he wants the entire event "Grover to go." So the entire clause *Grover to go* is the object of *want* and is unusual in that it is an infinitival (untensed) clause with a lexical subject (rather than PRO). It is interesting that, while *want* is such a common verb in English, verbs of this type are actually very rare in the world's languages. Hyams (1984) suggested that since verbs such as *want* have unusual structural properties, they should be learned late by English-speaking children. On the other hand, Limber (1973) and Bloom, Tackeff, and Lahey (1984) found that such verbs were among the first used by the children they studied. Eisenberg wanted to find out whether it was easier or harder for children to learn the structural properties of these verbs than other types.

4. *Try* and *pretend*, which can never be used with direct objects, so are always subject controlled, as in "Grover tried PRO to jump over the fence."

5. *Promise* and *threaten*, which are unusual in that they are subject controlled even when they appear with a direct object, as discussed above in connection with C. Chomsky's work.

6. *Say*, which is in a class by itself. It is also an exceptional control verb in that it requires arbitrary control of PRO. "Grover said PRO to jump over the fence" cannot mean that Grover will jump. *Say*, like *promise*, is an apparent exception to the principle that the closest c-commanding NP controls PRO, so Eisenberg suggested that it, too, would be acquired late.

Eisenberg used an elicited production task in which she attempted to elicit the production of sentences with infinitival complements from the child subjects by telling brief stories and inviting the child to complete them. For example, here is her story designed to elicit "Bert wants Mickey to find Ernie." Bert and Mickey dolls are standing; an Ernie doll is under the steps. The experimenter says, "Ernie is hiding (Bert doll looks for Ernie doll). Bert can't find Ernie." Bert doll says to Mickey doll, "Please find Ernie for me." The experimenter says, "Bert wants . . . . You finish the story. Bert . . ."

In addition to the elicited production task, Eisenberg used an act-out comprehension task. An interesting feature of the study was that although all 25 of the subjects were able to produce infinitival constructions, not one of them exhibited complete adult understanding of the control properties of all the verbs in the study. The children were much more likely to produce sentences without direct objects than with them, even when a sentence that is ungrammatical for an adult was the result. For instance, many of the children produced sentences such as "Bert tells to pick Mickey up," sometimes with the meaning that Bert will pick Mickey up and sometimes with the meaning that Ernie (not mentioned in the sentence) will do so. This is confirmation of the theory initially developed by McDaniel et al. (1990/1991) that for some children PRO takes arbitrary reference. Only the younger children produced sentences with *tell* without direct objects. Many more children (including the older ones) produced such sentences with the less familiar verb *force*. The reverse type of error did not occur, however. Direct objects were never used with verbs that do not allow them; there were no sentences such as "*Bert tries Mickey to fall." Eight of the children produced sentences with *for* as a complementizer, as frequently in incorrect (e.g., "*Ernie tells for him [Bert] to go to bed") as in correct (e.g., "Bert wants for Mickey to find Ernie") constructions.

Many children made the familiar error of taking *promise* to be an object control verb. *Say*, the other exceptional verb, also proved to be difficult for many children. Few of them restricted control to a character outside the sentence. Some required and others allowed subject control of sentences with *say*.

With respect to the *want* versus *tell* issue, results were mixed. Six of the children were apparently incorrectly treating *want* as a control verb, meaning that they had not yet learned the exceptional characteristic it has by which it takes an infinitive clause with a lexical subject as its complement. Another four children (who were among the youngest) seemed to have no problem with the exceptional character of *want*. The different behavior of these children, as well as the great individual differences found throughout the study, reinforces our appreciation of the different paths children take as they move toward an adult grammar and an adult lexicon.

Cairns et al. (1994a), in their longitudinal study of acquisition of control, used a number of different kinds of verbs in their sentences with infinitival complements to see whether children would abandon arbitrary reference for PRO at different times for different verbs. Their subject control verbs were *want, decide, try,* and *like*, as in "Grover wanted/decided/tried/liked PRO to jump over the fence." The object control verbs were *tell, pick, order,* and *choose*, as in "Grover told/picked/ordered/chose Bert PRO to jump over the fence." They found that there was no difference among the eight verbs. Recall that children were seen every 3 months. A child who was Grammar Type IA, with arbitrary control for infinitives, would demonstrate arbitrary control for both subject and object control sentences and for all eight verbs. At a later period, when that child matured and required control (either subject or object) for the infinitives, behavior would typically be uniform across all verbs. It was not the case that a child would, say, require obligatory control for *pick*, but allow arbitrary control for *tell*. These results suggest that children are very good at determining which verbs are members of a particular structural class.

While Eisenberg's (1989; Eisenberg & Cairns, 1994) study identifies much individual variation in the children's behavior across verb types, Cairns et al.'s (1994a) study points to uniformity within verb class. The fact that all the studies on acquisition of control find a great deal of individual variation in the ages at which children acquire obligatory control is further evidence for the kind of variation Eisenberg identified. The developmental scenario, then, is one in which the child discovers a structural feature of a verb, such as the fact that it takes an embedded clause as one of its arguments, and then quickly identifies verbs with similar syntactic properties. The initial discovery may take longer for some children than for others, but once made, the classification of verbs follows quickly. This fast classification may be facilitated if verbs that share structural features also share elements of meaning.

There are some verbs whose syntactic behavior has long presented a learnability puzzle to developmental psycholinguists. These are verbs that alternate between syntactic structures. The first type to be addressed in the literature was that class of verbs that undergo dative alternation. We can say either "John gave the book to Mary" or "John gave Mary the book." *Give*, then, is a verb that alternates between an NP to NP (prepositional) structure and an NP NP (double object) structure. This is known as dative alternation; the puzzle arises because all verbs that enter into the prepositional structure do not undergo dative alternation. We can say "Jane drove her car to Chicago," but not "*Jane drove Chicago her car." Baker addressed this issue first in 1979, and it has come to be called Baker's paradox. The question is: How do children come to learn exactly which verbs undergo dative alternation and which do not? This is exactly the same thing as asking how the distinction is maintained in the English language, because if children did not acquire the distinction, it would vanish in a generation.

We can think of two ways, in principle, that children could acquire the distinction, but both turn out to be empirically false. First, children could allow all the verbs that enter into the prepositional structure to undergo dative alternation and rely upon adults in the environment to provide negative evidence to identify which ones are incorrect. In other words, children could engage in overgeneralization from which they would need negative evidence to recover. Such overgeneralization would, of course, be a classical learnability paradox; we know that children cannot rely on negative evidence to acquire any features of language.

Second, children could do exactly the opposite and be extremely conservative learners. On this scenario, they would use verbs only in the prepositional structure until they heard adults producing the double object construction of individual verbs. They would then, based exclusively on that positive evidence, note in the lexicon that those verbs could undergo the dative alternation. Baker (1979), a theoretical linguist, assumed that this must be the way children acquire lexical information about verbs that undergo the dative alternation. However, the hypothesis that children are conservative learners has been called into question. Mazurkewich and White (1984) and Pinker (1984, 1991) and his colleagues (Gropen, Pinker, Hollander, Goldberg, & Wilson, 1989) have reported a great deal of data, both naturalistic and experimental, that children do, indeed, overgeneralize the dative alternation. For example, Gropen et al. (1989) taught experimental subjects nonsense verbs in the prepositional form, such as "The bear is pilking the pig to the giraffe" (where *pilking* meant pushing the pig in a gondola car to the giraffe), and in a test phase, when the children saw a tiger pilking a horse to a cat, they said of the cat, "The tiger is pilking him the horse."

If children overgeneralize the dative alternation and do not receive negative evidence to recover from incorrect generalizations, how do they manage to acquire an adultlike lexicon with respect to these verbs? Pinker (1991) provided a general solution to Baker's paradox by suggesting that the structure into which a verb enters is predictable by its meaning (which is connected to the structure by linking rules). Verbs that enter into the dative alternation have the meaning (in their prepositional form) "X causes Y to go to Z." In "John gave the book to Mary," John is X, the book is Y, and Mary is Z. The dative alternation changes them into verbs having the meaning "X causes Z to have Y," as in "John gave Mary the book." All verbs that undergo dative alternation belong to the broad *conflation class* (Pinker's term) of verbs whose meanings can alternate in just this way. We can see, now, why "Mary drove the car to Chicago" does not alternate with "*Mary drove Chicago the car." Chicago does not end up possessing the car, so the NP NP meaning of the alternation is not satisfied.

Things are made more difficult, however, because not all members of this broad conflation class undergo dative alternation. Here is a very elegant example. We can say "John kicked the box to Mary" or "John kicked Mary the box," and we can say "John pulled the box to Mary," but we cannot say "*John pulled Mary the box." Why is that? Both involve John causing Mary to have the box. According to Pinker (1991), it is because English has the peculiar characteristic of only allowing the narrow subclass of verbs that "denote instantaneous imparting of force to an object causing ballistic physical motion ('throw,' 'toss,' 'kick,' etc.) to be given a new meaning, roughly to cause someone to possess an object by means of instantaneously imparting force to it" (p. 102). It does not apply to seemingly similar verbs, such as those whose definitions involve continuous exertion of force (*pull, push, carry*, etc.). These subsets of broad conflation classes of verbs are known as "narrow conflation classes" (or "conflation subclasses"). The semantic information associated with broad conflation classes is not sufficient to determine which verbs will undergo alternations. They state the necessary semantic conditions for the verb to alternate, but it is the narrow subclasses (or more precisely the narrow-range rules that apply to the verbs in those subclasses) that define the actual existence of alternating verbs.

Pinker (1991) suggested that many of children's overgeneralization errors occur because children acquire the general definition of the broad conflation class of verbs to which the dative alternation can apply and then incorrectly apply broad-range rules, allowing some verbs to alternate when they should not. This does not present a learnability problem, however, because children do not actually mark such verbs in their lexicons as alternating verbs; thus, they do not need negative evidence to "unlearn" them. They simply mark them as possible alternators without actually classifying them as such in the lexicon. The broad-range rules, then, allow children to be creative without cluttering up their lexicons with incorrect information. (Pinker suggested that adults, too, use broad-range rules creatively. He cited many examples, such as "Can you explain me language breakdown?") The child's task is to pay careful attention to the semantics of the verbs she hears and figure out what the ones that alternate have in common. This is done fairly conservatively, as the child develops nuances of verb meanings and classifies verbs along narrow semantic dimensions. Finally, she will be in a position to formulate narrow-range rules and actually mark as alternating only those verbs that are semantically identical to those she has heard alternate. This, then, gives rise to yet another kind of generalization—the correct generalization of narrow-range rules to new verbs that are members of the narrow subclass. This is similar to the proposals put forth by Fodor (1985), except that she denied the necessity to postulate the second kind of generalization and insisted that children are completely conservative learners. Although they may experiment with verbs from the broad conflation class, they mark as alternating only those verbs they have actually heard alternate. Fodor's proposal has the advantage that it does not require children to rely on remarkably subtle semantic judgments.

Another example of verb structure that is conditioned by its meaning is the passive. Again, there is an alternation between active and passive structures that some verbs enter into but others do not. We can say "The girl loves the cat" and "The cat is loved by the girl," and we can say "The salami weighs five pounds," but not "*Five pounds is weighed by the salami." Pinker, Lebeaux, and Frost (1987) adduced both naturalistic and experimental evidence that children are not conservative learners of the passive alternation, but overgeneralize new verbs freely, if they are first learned in the active form, to the passive construction. Again, we have the learnability paradox that Pinker et al. (1987) solved by suggesting that all verbs that undergo the passive alternation have a similar meaning in their active version. It is that there is an *agent* that performs an action upon a *patient* (the recipient of the action). These are known as the *thematic roles* attached to a verb. That patient (or recipient of the action) becomes the subject of the passive sentence, and the actor appears in the *by* phrase (or it can be omitted altogether, in which case a truncated passive is the result). It is clear, then, why it is grammatical to say "The cat is loved by the girl" but not "*Five pounds is weighed by the salami." There is no sense in which the salami is performing an action, the recipient of which is the five pounds.

English does not restrict passivization to verbs denoting action on a patient by an agent, however. We can also alternate "The blanket covered the baby" and "The baby was covered by the blanket." Pinker et al. (1987) suggested that these are those classes of verbs in which the thematic roles of agent and patient are construed abstractly. The blanket, while not able to perform an independent action, is metaphorically construed as doing so when it is said to cover the baby. Thus, the passive alternation is allowed. Children first acquire the most general, core semantic requirement. This prediction was confirmed in an experiment reported by Pinker et al., in which children were more likely to produce the passive version of actional nonsense verbs having heard only the active version, than they were of nonactional, "spatial" nonsense verbs. The actional verbs meant "to leapfrog over," "to knock over," "to slide down the back of," and "to rub the head of." The nonactional verbs meant "to be at the center of," "to be at the end of," "to be hanging from," and "to be wrapped around." In that experiment there were two groups of children, one 3 years to 4 years, 5 months, and an older group 4 years, 5 months, to 5 years, 5 months. The two groups were equal in the proportion of passives they produced for the action verbs, but very different in their production of passives for the nonaction verbs. The younger group produced virtually no passives, whereas the older children produced as many as they did for the action verbs. It appears as though younger children restrict their generalization of the passive to these verbs that fit the semantic core meaning, whereas the older children are more experimental and are willing to extend the passive to the more metaphorical construal, which allows some nonactional verbs to passivize.

The theory that a verb's semantics determines its structural representation relies on the existence of linking rules to map the elements of semantic structure onto syntactic structure. The existence of linking rules has been demonstrated by Gropen, Pinker, Hollander, and Goldberg (1991) in a series of experiments addressing yet another type of verbal alternation. Called the *locative alternation*, it is illustrated by the fact that we can say "John loaded hay into the truck" and also "John loaded the truck with hay." Not all verbs undergo this alternation, however; we say "John poured water into the glass" but not "*John poured the glass with water." It also works the other way around, as we can say "John filled the glass with water" but not "*John filled water into the glass." Gropen et al. (1991; following Pinker, 1991, and Rappaport & Levin, 1985, 1988) pointed out that it is the verb's semantics that determines its structure. In each case there is one argument of the verb that is its "main event," and it is realized as the direct object. The verb *pour* means that liquid goes down in a steady stream, so the streaming of the water is the main event connected with pour. One can pour a liquid onto anything or into any sort of vessel, so the fact that water is poured into a glass is irrelevant to the primary meaning of *pour*. The presence of water (or any liquid), however, is essential for the main event to be fulfilled. Therefore, *water* appears as the direct object of *pour*. Conversely, the main event of *fill* is that the interior of some vessel is caused to completely contain something. It doesn't have to be water; it could be sand or marbles or anything. Thus, the glass is essential to the main event of *fill*, but *water* is not, so *the glass* appears as the direct object of *fill*. This is an example of a linking rule, by which elements of verb meanings get mapped onto syntactic structures. In the case of *load*, it isn't so much that *load* alternates as it is that its main event can be construed either as an activity that applies to the substance being loaded (in which case *hay* will appear as the direct object) or as an activity that applies to the receptical (in which case *truck* will appear as a direct object).

Gropen et al. (1991) reported experiments with children between the ages of 3 years, 4 months, and 5 years, 11 months, in which they taught the children nonsense verbs that focused on either the manner of action, such as *pour*, or on the resulting state effected by the action, such as *fill*. The former involved a zig-zagging motion, the latter an activity that changed the color of a surface. During the teaching phase of the experiment, the novel words were produced in completely neutral (and identical) syntactic frames (e.g., "Let me show you what *keating* is," or "When I do this, it's called *keating*"). In the test phase, the children were asked to use the new verb to describe the experimenter's actions. The results were dramatic and highly significant statistically. Children used the verbs whose main event was the manner of motion in the *pour* type of construction, and the ones whose end state constituted the main event in the *fill* type of construction. The experimenters, then, strongly influenced the syntactic constructions that children assigned to novel verbs, although they presented them with no distinguishing syntactic, only with semantic, information.

The locative alternation is another example, then, of the intimate relationship between a verb's semantics and its syntax. Not surprisingly, there are subclasses within the general broad conflation class of verbs undergoing the alternation (Gropen et al., 1989; Pinker, 1991). It is clear that this relationship between syntax and semantics provides for a complex interaction in the acquisition of verbs. Once a child has acquired the semantic distinctions that relate to the linking rules, she can produce novel sentences that will be grammatically correct if she properly construes the meaning of the verbs involved. Furthermore, she can use syntactic bootstrapping (as described by Gleitman, 1990) to discover the semantic distinctions in the first place by determining the semantic commonalities among verbs linked to similar syntactic constructions.

Although the syntactic behavior of many verbs may follow from their semantic representation, there are other syntactic phenomena for which this is not the case. For instance, in English there are some transitive verbs that require a direct object, whereas there are others after which the direct object can be omitted (if it is understood from context). Many of the verbs that allow the direct object to be omitted, such as *eat* ("John ate lunch yesterday" or "John ate yesterday"), are very similar in meaning to verbs that do not, such as *devour* ("John devoured lunch yesterday" but not "*John devoured yesterday").

Verbs with omissible objects are quite common in English, as are verbs that do not allow the object to be omitted. Children must eventually distinguish between the two in their lexicons. Now reconsider, for this type of verb, the learnability paradox initially presented by the alternating verbs discussed above. If children overgeneralize the omission of objects with verbs for which that is incorrect in English, then the only way they could recover from the overgeneralization is through negative evidence, which they do not receive. Only if they are conservative learners, omitting objects only from those verbs after which their caretakers have omitted objects, will they avoid errors from which they could not recover. Pinker (1991) argued that children overgeneralize the verbs that enter into the locative alternation, but escape the learnability problem because the verbs fall into conflation subclasses defined by their semantic representations, which in turn correspond to their syntactic behavior. As Ingham (1993/1994) pointed out, however, a solution based on the meanings of verbs will not work with omissible object verbs. They share no similarity of meaning that is distinct from the meaning of the verbs after which objects cannot be omitted. Omissibility of objects is a purely syntactic characteristic of verbs, with no relationship to the verbs' semantic representations. Thus, Ingham predicted that children would have to be conservative learners of this verb type, and he conducted two very clever studies to test his prediction.

Before describing his studies, let us review what is meant by conservative learning. It simply means that the child will assume (represent in the lexicon) that transitive verbs must be followed by a direct object until she hears an adult use the verb with an "understood" object that is not spoken. For example, the conservative learning child would say "Dolly eating cookie" and "Dolly eating carrot" until she hears an exchange such as "Where's Fred?" "Oh, he's eating." Then the child will adjust her lexical representation of *eat* and be able to say "Dolly eating." However, she will not generalize the object omission to other verbs, such as *follow*, until she hears someone say something like "Daddy ran to the train and Jimmy followed."

Ingham (1993/1994) reported two studies, one naturalistic and one experimental. In the former he examined the match between a child's use of verbs with and without direct objects and that of her mother, when the child (Naomi) was between the ages of 1 year, 10 months, and 1 year, 11 months. The mother omitted the objects from those verbs that took optional objects 20% of the time; so did Naomi. Naomi omitted objects only 4.8% of the time, however, following verbs from which her mother never omitted the object. The difference in percentages is highly significant statistically and quite consistent with the hypothesis that Naomi was a conservative learner.

In Ingham's experiment, he taught nonsense verbs to two groups of 4-year-olds. The verbs were transitive, describing an action performed on Play Dough. For example, *mivving* could mean that Play Dough was being pressed into thin strips using a garlic press. One group heard a number of sentences like "The puppet is mivving the Play Dough," all of which had a direct object after *mivving*. The other group heard the sentences in two forms, half with the direct object and the other half without, as in "The puppet is mivving." Thus, for the second group, the object was identified as optional, whereas for the first group it was not. After the presentations, the children were simply asked (when the puppet was performing the action) "What is the puppet doing?" The results were quite dramatic. The group who had heard the verb used with the optional object omitted it 64% of the time in the test phase of the experiment. The other group omitted it only 20% of the time. This difference suggests that in a simple experimental situation, the children are conservative learners of new words.

The fact that children cannot rely on negative evidence when they learn the structural properties of verbs leads to some very general predictions about lexical learning. If the syntactic properties of the verbs are predictable from their semantic representations, then overgeneralization is safe, and we should not be surprised to observe it among some children. If, on the other hand, the structural properties are purely syntactic, there is no way to recover from overgeneralization, and children should be conservative learners for all such verb classes. A major question, of course, is how do children know the difference, in advance. How do they know that it is safe to overgeneralize passive and locative alternations, but not omissible objects? Perhaps they do not actually know in advance, but as they hear verbs that undergo various syntactic operations, they search for similar semantic properties among them. Only if they find such properties will they feel safe to make some generalizations. If they find none, they will not.

Acquisition of Adjectives

Adjectives, like verbs, enter into control structures containing PRO and have syntactic properties that determine their referents. The only difference between the sentences "John is eager to please" and "John is easy to please" is the adjectives *eager* and *easy*, yet in the former it is John who will be doing the pleasing and in the latter some unnamed character is pleasing John. A number of linguists have studied these sentence types and have put forth a number of different analyses of them. (For a nice review, see McKee, Cripe, & Campos, 1995.) An investigation of children's interpretation of these adjectives was another focus of C. Chomsky's (1969) study. She showed her subjects a blindfolded doll and asked whether the doll was hard or easy to see. Whatever their answer, she asked them to reverse the situation. Many of her subjects, some over 8 years, reported that the doll was hard to see and to make her easy to see you must remove her blindfold. Chomsky interpreted this error in terms of the Minimum Distance Principle (MDP), which she was investigating. "The doll is easy/hard to see" violates the principle in that the subject of the infinitive is not the closest NP. In fact, the closest NP is the object of the infinitive, and the subject is not mentioned. Thus, the children err by interpreting the sentence in accordance with the MDP, which leads to a misinterpretation.

Cromer (1970) noted that Chomsky had tricked her subjects by showing them a blindfolded doll. To answer correctly, by saying that the doll is easy to see, they would have to ignore the highly salient blindfold and realize that it was completely irrelevant to their answer. Thus, Cromer, using hand puppets, did a systematic study of object-type adjectives such as "The wolf is easy to bite," subject-type adjectives such as "The wolf is eager to bite," and ambiguous adjectives such as "The wolf is nice to bite," which can receive either subject or object interpretation. Some of his subjects performed exactly like Chomsky's, interpreting all the sentences as though the wolf was the subject of the infinitive. Another group (all above the age of 6 1/2) produced adult interpretations. Yet another group gave mixed responses to all three sentence types. These findings were generally interpreted as indicating that young children lack the grammatical ability to provide a structural analysis of sentences with object-type adjectives.

A more recent study (McKee et al., 1995) called into question the claim that young children lack the grammatical capacity to analyze correctly sentences with object-type verbs. Using a picture selection task, the researchers elicited responses from children aged 1 year, 11 months, to 5 years, 11 months, to sentences with four object-type adjectives (*easy, hard, impossible,* and *difficult*) and ambiguous adjectives (*dirty, big, nice,* and *old*). Thus, their children were much younger than those studied in previous research; there was also a group of adult subjects. They found that the 2- and 3-year-olds did give significantly fewer object responses to the sentences with object-type adjectives than did the 4- and 5-year-olds (who did not differ significantly from the adults); however, even the youngest children did produce a great number of object responses, to the ambiguous sentences as well as the unambiguous ones. Furthermore, there was an interaction between age and adjective type; the youngest children exhibited differential responses to the four object-type adjectives. McKee et al. interpreted these results as demonstrating that even the very young children have the *grammatical* capacity to analyze such sentences, but their failure to do so arises from incomplete lexical information regarding the structural properties of the adjectives themselves. It will be interesting if future research in this area focuses on the relationship between children's input with respect to adjectives of this type and their lexical acquisition of their structural properties.

Just as relational verbs, such as *come* and *go*, create difficulty for children acquiring vocabulary, so do adjectives that mean different things depending upon the relational context in which they occur. Thus, a shot glass is small for adults, but may be large in the context of a doll's tea party. Using this very distinction, Carey (reported in de Villiers & de Villiers, 1978) demonstrated that 2- and 3-year-old children have an absolute notion of *little* and claim that the shot glass is little in all contexts, whereas 4- and 5-year-olds were able to explain that the glass was little for themselves but big for the dolls.

Adjectives that define the dimensions of objects are, like relational words of all kinds, acquired imperfectly at the beginning of vocabulary development (Carey, 1982; Clark, 1972). Various experimental methodologies have revealed similar orderings of pairs of adjectives in terms of the ease with which children acquire control over the contrasts they encode. Easiest is the *big–little* contrast, with children around the age of 4 being in complete control of the contrast that pair represents. The contrasts *tall–short, long–short,* and *high–low* are acquired next, followed by *thick–thin* and *wide–narrow. Deep–shallow* is the latest acquired contrast reported in this literature. *More* and *less* are also not discriminated by 3-year-olds (Donaldson & Balfour, 1968). Clark (1983) suggested that initially both terms simply mean "amount" to the child, their relational meanings being acquired later.

Acquisition of Function Words

Function words, or closed class words, are extremely important in language learning because they serve a largely grammatical function. These are articles, prepositions, conjunctions, auxiliaries, quantifiers, and so forth. Bates et al. (1994), in the study cited above, reported that the incidence of function words in children's speech remains constant and low until their vocabulary reaches around 400 words, roughly around the age of 2 1/2, and then increases proportionally. There is good reason to believe, however, that children have lexical and structural representations of function words long before they actually use them. Shipley, Smith, and Gleitman (1969) showed that children who are not using function words respond better to sentences containing them than to those without them. Gerken and McIntosh (1993, 1995) showed that normally developing 2-year-olds and language disordered 3- and 4-year-olds perform better on a picture identification task if asked to "Find the bird for me" than if asked to "Find bird for me" or "Find gub bird for me." Both these groups of children rarely produced articles in their spontaneous speech. The importance of being able to identify function words cannot be overemphasized. One of the central issues of language acquisition is how the child begins, in infancy, to "get into" the continuous speech stream and identify word and phrasal boundaries. The fact that function words have different prosodic characteristics from content words and identify the onset of phrases makes them of paramount importance in this primary language-learning period.

In a well-known study of very young children, Katz, Baker, and Macnamara (1974) demonstrated that 17-month-old children already have a distinction between common and proper nouns and can discriminate them by the presence or absence of an article. Common nouns, but not proper nouns, are preceded by an article. If I show you an unusual sort of cat and say "That's a Bianca," you will think that Bianca is a type of cat (a common noun); but if I say "That's Bianca," you will think that is the cat's name. Katz et al. did exactly this with their infant subjects. They introduced the children to a new doll and said either "This is Dax" or "This is a Dax." During a test phase, there was another similar doll present. When asked to "Show me Dax (or a Dax)" the children who had heard the name preceded by an article picked up either the original doll or the similar one. The others selected only the originally named doll.

Maratsos (1976) demonstrated that 3- and 4-year-olds appreciated the definite–indefinite distinction for articles. The definite article is *the* and it is used when referring to a specific noun that has already been introduced into the discourse context; the indefinite article *a* is used when a character is first introduced or when the speaker does not wish to refer to a specific character. For instance, if we are talking and I refer to "the woman," it must refer to a specific person in the discourse known to us both; "a woman," on the other hand, can refer to any woman and, in fact, cannot refer to a female in our discourse context. In one of Maratsos's experiments, he showed his subjects a picture of three dogs, each in a car, with a boy talking to one of them. Then the child was told either "Then suddenly the dog drove away" or "Then suddenly a dog drove away." The children were then asked which dog drove away. Those who had heard the definite article chose the dog the boy had been talking to, whereas those who heard the indefinite article selected one of the other two dogs.

Relational words constitute special problems for the young child. Deictic words such as *here–there* and *this–that* obviously have different meanings depending upon the location of the speaker and listener (Clark & Senegul, 1978; de Villiers & de Villiers, 1974). Locatives tend to be easier than demonstratives, and the words indicating near perspective (*this* and *here*) tend to be easier than those indicating far perspective. These contrasts are first mastered when the child uses herself as the point of reference, but it is not until fairly late childhood that the meanings of these words are controlled when they are used by a second person with a perspective different from that of the child. Wales (1986) reported that fewer than half of the 7-year-olds in his study had the full deictic contrast with shifting reference points. Similar effects are found for relational prepositions, such as *in front of*. Children typically first understand this expression with reference only to themselves, then to objects with obvious fronts and backs, and only later to objects in which the front and back is dependent upon the perspective of the speaker (Kuczaj & Maratsos, 1975).

Quantifiers are similar to relational words in the sense that they can take on variable meanings. These are words such as *every, each, all,* and *some.* Consider the sentence "Every boy loves his mother." This can mean either that all of the boys in a group love one boy's mother (the collective meaning) or that each of the boys loves his own mother (the distributive meaning). Roeper and de Villiers (1990) have shown that children as young as 4 can provide both interpretations for sentences with *every*. However, they also have reported an interesting nonadult phenomenon that they call *quantifier spreading*. If a child is shown a picture of three bears, each of which is wearing a hat, she will answer "yes" (as would an adult) to the question "Is every bear wearing a hat?" But if there is an extra hat in the picture as well, many children will point to the hat and answer "No, not that one" (Philip & Aurelio, 1990). This is not a newly discovered phenomenon; years ago, Inhelder and Piaget (1964) gave it a cognitive explanation. It is the focus of a good deal of current research in developmental psycholinguistics. Crain et al. (1995) have called the phenomenon into question, and Utakis (1995) has suggested that it is related to the acquisition of Principle B.

Conjunctions are among the most important function words in that they have profound implications for the development of the child's syntactic system. In the discussion of the acquisition of principles of control, I argued that the discovery that some conjunctions require the subordination of clauses, whereas others allow them to be coordinated, is what triggers the child's movement into adult analyses of sentences containing PRO. Cairns, McDaniel, Hsu, and Rapp (1994), in their longitudinal study, employed three different kinds of temporal subordinating conjunctions, *before, after,* and *while.* They found (as they had with the verbs in infinitive sentences) that all three conjunctions were classified as subordinating at the same time for each of the children in their study. This is another example, then, of children rapidly acquiring structural information about all the words in a particular grammatical class. Although children discover at widely variable ages that such conjunctions are not coordinating, once that discovery is made, it extends to all the temporal subordinating conjunctions.

Before and *after* were among the relational words studied long ago (Clark, 1971). It was discovered that children would interpret sentences such as "The horse kicked the pig after he jumped over the fence" in terms of the temporal order of mention of events in the sentence, rather than with reference to the temporal meaning of the conjunction. Children would enact this sentence, for instance, with the horse first kicking the pig, then jumping over the fence. Clark and Senegul (1978) demonstrated that children exhibit knowledge of the

relational meaning of *before* and *after* when they are used as prepositions earlier than when they are used as subordinating conjunctions.
Hsu (1981; Hsu, Cairns, & Fiengo, 1985) discovered that some of her
subjects knew the structural properties of the conjunctions without
demonstrating knowledge of the relational aspect of their meaning.
This is an important finding, because it shows that some aspects of the
meaning of words can be dissociated from their structural properties.

CHAPTER 6

Using Language

In the previous chapters I have presented a conceptualization of language as the biologically based communication system of humans. It is unlike the communication systems of other animals in that it is far more complex; it is characterizable by abstract, formal representations; and it is far more flexible. Different human groups use different variants of human language, whereas the communication systems of most other species are uniform across each species. Ours is similar to the communication systems of other animals, however, in that its neurological and anatomical roots are genetically encoded products of the evolution of the species, and its development in the young of the species is the result of the interaction of those genetically based systems and the external environment.

So far in this book, I have addressed primarily the linguistic tools the child develops to create structured collections of words that carry meaning. This has involved descriptions of morphological, syntactic, and lexical development. In this chapter I examine two very different abilities that are a result of the child's acquisition of those tools to create sentences. One is the ability of the child to actually use those created sentences in communication. The other is the child's ability to think about and reflect on those linguistic tools as explicitly distinct from their use in communication—known as metalinguistic skill. It is almost certainly the case that, while we share with other animals the ability to communicate, only we can consciously reflect upon our communication system.

Finally, the most important part of this chapter addresses the relationship of all three of these factors to the child's ability to learn to read. To do this, the child must have an intact linguistic system, the discourse and narrative skills required for effective communication, and the metalinguistic skills to perceive the language as an object that can have a written representation. In the last two decades, developmental psycholinguistics has had two applications on which it has had a major impact. One has been on our understanding of language disorders of children; the other has been on our understanding of developing literacy.

In the first chapter of this book, I developed the idea that language is a modular system, separate from general cognition and from social usage. In the same way, language (in the sense of grammar and vocabulary) is separable from general communication, and both are separable from metalinguistic skills. For instance, we know that there are children who have greatly impaired language but good communication skills—Genie (Curtiss, 1977; Curtiss, Fromkin, Krashen, Rigler, & Rigler, 1974), for instance, and many children with language disorders. It appears, however, that the ability to learn to read requires a fully mature grammar and good metalinguistic skills. This is why it is not uncommon for a subtle, undiagnosed language disorder to be discovered because a child is having difficulty learning to read. Children with specific language impairment often have problems in both pragmatic (Leonard, 1994) and metalinguistic (Menyuk, 1991) skill. They also usually have difficulty learning to read.

Metalinguistic skill and general communicative skill are also separable, especially in the early years of language acquisition. Children of 2, 3, or even 4 years may be able to communicate with language quite normally, yet be unable to judge the grammaticality of a sentence or tell someone what word would result if you remove the /s/ sound from the word *spin*. Both of these abilities, however, are important predictors of a child's ability to do well in first-grade reading class. We need, then, to examine these two abilities separately, as we have examined grammar and vocabulary separately. Only then will we be in a position to address the relevance of all three to developing literacy.

Acquisition of Communication Skills

When we think of the child's acquisition of communication skills, we think primarily of the development of conversational skills. However, conversation fits into the general concept of "text," which, according to Halliday and Hasan (1976), includes spoken or written passages, monologues, and dialogues. We can, then, ask not only what children talk about and how they structure early conversations, but also what linguistic devices they use to construct coherent and cohesive texts.

One way of approaching the question of what children talk about is to look at the communicative uses to which the child puts the utterances he produces. This way of analyzing early speech is modeled on an analysis of adult speech suggested by Austin (1962) and Searle (1969), among others, in a theory of speech acts. They noted that some utterances (called *performatives*) do not make an assertion, but themselves perform an act. "I promise to take out the garbage" is such an utterance. Other sentences may have a literal meaning when taken out of context that does not obtain when that sentence becomes an utterance in a communicative context. The sentence "It is cold in this room" can be a simple statement of fact; however, uttered by one person to another in a drafty room, it can function as an indirect request to close the window or bring a sweater. Often the nonliteral use of language requires shared knowledge between the speaker and the hearer before communication can be successful. This is required, for instance, for the perception of sarcasm without intonational cues. It is important, then, to ask what the functions of early language are and how children come to use and understand the nonliteral use of language.

Numerous investigators have chosen different descriptive categories to characterize the functions of early language. Halliday (1973, 1975) noted seven functions that appeared before the age of 2: instrumental, regulatory, interactional, personal, heuristic, imaginative, and informative. Dore (1974) identified a series of primitive speech acts associated with the one-word stage of language acquisition. These were labeling, repeating, answering, requesting action, requesting answer, calling, greeting, protesting, and practicing. It is easy to see that there is no conceptual conflict between these two descriptive systems, as they describe a similar range of behaviors. As the child ages, new speech acts emerge (Dore, Gearhart, & Newman, 1978) and by the age of 3, utterances expressing descriptions and assertions, regulative and conversational devices, and performatives are observed. Furthermore, the instances of each type of function increase with age. The requesting function, for instance, in the speech of the 3-year-old includes "yes–no" questions, who questions, action and permission requests, and process questions and suggestions, representing a major advance beyond the one-word stage of primitive speech acts.

Garvey (1975) classified requests coded with *want* and *need* to be inferred requests, but true indirect requests do not appear until the end of the second or the beginning of the third year, with utterances such as "Where is the truck?" used as a request for the truck, and *could you* and *would you* by yet older children. Oblique indirect requests (hints) are not attested until early school age. Anderson (1978) investigated the use of indirect requests of various types used during role playing in children between the ages of 4 and 7, and found that more indirect requests were used when the children were playing the role of parent than when they were playing the role of child.

Turning to the comprehension of indirect requests, Shatz (1978) found that 2-year-olds do not discriminate between requests for action and requests for *information*. Some evidence, however, indicates that some indirect directives are responded to correctly by 3-year-olds (Dore, 1977; Reeder, 1980), although there is some question as to how indirect these statements really are (Ervin-Tripp, 1977). Leonard, Wilcox, Fulmer, and Dans (1978) and Meier (1981) have shown an age progression in the degree of indirectness that children are able to tolerate and still interpret the statement as a request. Meier presented 8-, 10-, and 12-year-olds with indirect requests of varying levels of indirectness. For instance, for a directive to wash his face, a child in a story was told either "Your face needs washing," "What a dirty face," "I have some soap," or "Next time, leave some dirt for me." Children of all ages responded to the first two types of statement as if they were requests; there was a dramatic increase in request responses to the third type in the 10-year-olds and to the fourth type in the 12-year-olds.

A great deal of attention has been given to the development of conversational abilities in the child. To participate in a successful conversation, the interlocutors must know how to take turns in speaking and how to maintain a topic or change it when the situation warrants. Conversational interaction requires the ability to assess the communicative needs of the hearer based on knowledge of shared information.

Precursors of conversational interchanges can be observed in prelinguistic interactions such as peek-a-boo games. Stern, Jaffe, Beebe, and Bennett (1975), in a study of 3- and 4-month-old infants and their mothers, noted that they engage in turn-taking in vocalizations and also engage in frequent mutual eye contact. Real conversational abilities, however, seem to begin around the age of 2, although at a very primitive level. By then, turn-taking is established, and the child's replies are frequently semantically related to the adult's utterances, although either no response or an inappropriate response is common (Garvey, 1975). Authors such as Snow (1977) and Shatz (1983) have observed that adults speaking with children focus primarily on maintenance of the conversation, rather than a true exchange of information. In studies of conversation between children of similar ages, Liberman and Garvey (1977) found that 3 1/2-year-old children have longer gaps (silence) between their conversational turns than adults do (an average of 1.2 seconds, compared with adults' .40 seconds). Older children have shorter gaps, but overlaps were rare. McTear (1985), however, shows that 4- and 5-year-olds have numerous overlaps, interrupting to grab a conversational turn more frequently than younger children do.

Foster (1985, 1986, 1990) (now Foster-Cohen) has studied topic initiation and maintenance extensively. She has reported that the earliest kind of topic to be initiated is what she calls *self topics* in which the child is the focus of attention. Next are *environmental topics*, which are introduced by gestures and vocalizations directed toward items in the environment. These early initiation strategies are typical of the end of the first year and become progressively more sophisticated during the second year of life, as the child begins to be able to use words to initiate topics. Toward the end of the second year, however, the child initiates topics that draw the adult's attention to something intangible. This type of initiation requires words to draw the adult's attention to whom has given the child a particular toy, who usually sits in a particular chair, and so forth. With the advent of word use, the child is also able to introduce topics that are not present in the discourse environment. Early topic maintenance is very brief, but can be enhanced by a cooperative adult who extends the topic over a series of similar conversational turns, such as in a naming game.

A crucial aspect of using language for communication in child or adult is an awareness of the information available to one's interlocutor. Before the age of 2, children typically do not seem to realize the necessity for making sure that they have the attention of another before they begin speaking. In 2-year-olds, however, attention-getting devices frequently precede vocalization. Research on the awareness of shared information produces widely varying results, however. On the one hand, recall that children as young as 5 (Maratsos, 1973) know the difference between use of the definite and indefinite articles. They know that the definite article *the* carries with it the presupposition that an object exists and that its existence is known to both speaker and hearer. The indefinite article *a* or *an*, however, carries no such presupposition. Even children beyond the age of 5, however, do not do well on various types of "communication games" that have been invented to investigate communicative abilities in children. Typically, these games will require the child to describe a picture to an adult (or to another child) who is behind a screen. Even with correction, children below the age of 6 or 7 do not accomplish this task with a high degree of success (Krauss & Glucksberg, 1977). It is not the case, however, that children have no sensitivity to the communicative needs of listeners. As Shatz and Gelman (1973) found, even 4-year-olds speak differently to 2-year-olds than they do to peers or adults. It is tempting to conclude that very young children have some knowledge that the needs of their listeners must be taken into account in the communication enterprise, but only older children can judge with a high degree of accuracy exactly what elements of information are actually needed by the hearer. However, recent work by Anderson, Clark, and Mullin (1991, 1994) suggests that this is probably not the way we should think about the situation.

Anderson et al. (1994) conducted extensive investigations of communicative interaction in children aged 7 to 13. They reported conversational interactions in which information givers and information receivers were given similar (but not identical) maps; the former was to communicate to the latter a particular path that he should draw on the map. (Of course, they could not see one another's maps.) Successful communication was measured by simply comparing the path drawn by the information receiver and the one intended by the information giver. They identified a number of interactional strategies employed by the most successful communicators. For instance, explicit probing to ascertain areas of shared knowledge was a feature of the good communicators. Equal numbers of questions were asked by good and poor communicators, but the crucial difference between them was that the successful communicators answered the questions, whereas the poor ones tended to ignore them. The good communicators, furthermore, could both identify problem points, at which communication was breaking down, and deal with them. Thus, successful communication was identified as an interactive enterprise, not simply the ability of a sole speaker to convey information (as is the case in many of the "communication games").

The most striking finding of the Anderson et al. studies is that, although there is a slight age trend associated with communicative success, there is enormous variability within each age group studied. For example, 25% of the 7-year-olds performed better than the average for the 13-year-olds, and (what is truly alarming) 25% of the 13-year-olds' scores were lower than the average for the 7-year-olds. (It is unfortunate that no adults participated in this study.) The authors pointed out that their data seem to be in sharp contrast to a wide array of studies that indicate children as young as 2 1/2 have an understanding of communication failure and a repertoire of behaviors to overcome those breakdowns (Bates, Camioni, & Volterra, 1979; Gallagher, 1991; Golinkoff, 1986). The distinction, they argued, is in whether children are engaged in conversational activity for social or for communicative purposes. Brown and Yule (1983) distinguished between *transactional* discourse, in which communicating information is the main purpose, and *interactional* discourse, which serves primarily a social function. What develops early and successfully is the child's social conversational abilities, not his communicative skills.

Support for the Anderson et al. (1994) position can be found in the work of Snow (1977) and Shatz (1983) (mentioned above), who suggested that the reason very young children acquire such good turn-taking skills is because caretakers are primarily concerned with maintenance of the conversation, rather than the exchange of information. Olsen-Fulero (1982) and Demetras, Post, and Snow (1986) showed that adults' use of devices such as questions and requests for clarification are designed mainly to maintain interaction with the child, rather than to effect information exchange. McTear (1987) reported that when children respond to requests for information clarification, adults are highly tolerant of ambiguous or underspecified responses. Thus, the child's early experience is directed toward the acquisition of social rather than true communicative interaction. We might also speculate that the social role of communication systems in human society is in general probably far more important than the communication of precise information (which was required in the Anderson et al. experiment). Thus, the social aspects of communication would be much more strongly biologically determined than would information transfer, which might need to be specifically taught. Recall from the work of Goldin-Meadow and Mylander (1990) that deaf children who are not exposed to gestural communication systems develop their own *home signs* as means of social interaction. The internal pressure to communicate socially is profound. The Anderson et al. work makes clear the importance of distinguishing between transactional and interactional aspects of children's conversation. It also has major implications for people who work with children in educational settings.

The final aspect of children's communication we need to address is the organization of *texts* (in Halliday's, 1975, sense). Whether the text is a narrative or a conversation, it must possess two important characteristics to be comprehensible and appropriate. It must be *coherent*, and it must be *cohesive*. Coherence refers to the fact that elements of the text, such as conversational turns, must be relevant to the rest of the conversation. Entire stretches of conversation are "about" something. Foster (1981, 1986, 1990) identified two kinds of relevance that go on simultaneously during a conversation. First is *horizontal relevance*, which refers to the coherence of consecutive utterances in a conversation. The other is *vertical relevance*, each utterance's relevance to the overall conversational topic. Children honor both kinds of coherence in early conversation. Bloom, Rocissano, and Hood (1976) studied linguistic devices by which their subjects, from 1 year, 9 months, to 3 years of age, expressed the contingency (horizontal relevance) between pairs of utterances. The devices were more sophisticated for the older than for the younger children, beginning with a simple elaboration of the adult's comment, and extending to full sentential responses to adult questions.

Whereas coherence refers to the general relevance of elements of a text to each other and to the topic of the text, cohesion refers to the specific linguistic devices that create connections between sentences. Coherence and cohesiveness, although distinct, are obviously highly related (Lilez, 1985). Texts with a high number of cohesive elements are usually judged to be more coherent than texts with less cohesion. Halliday and Hasan (1976) identified a number of cohesive devices, among them repetition of words and phrases, which can occur either in answers to questions or in statements that repeat an element from a previous utterance. The same kind of cohesion is attained in elliptical responses that assume the previous utterance, as in "Who was getting chased?" "The sheep." An important kind of cohesive device is reference of various kinds, either of lexical noun phrases ("A firetruck drove up to the front of the house. The *firemen* got out") or of pronouns ("Let's have some candy." "Okay, I'll get *some*").

A critical cohesive device that has been the subject of a great deal of study is the use of personal or possessive pronouns to refer to a character in the discourse context. The misuse of pronouns can, of course, have the opposite effect, of inhibiting the cohesive nature of a text. Klecan-Aker and Lopez (1985), Karmiloff-Smith (1986), and Shapiro and Hudson (1991), among others, have investigated the pervasive phenomenon of ambiguous reference, in which a child produces a pronoun (either a conversation or a narrative) whose referent cannot be uniquely determined. King and Rentel (1981) mentioned another kind of pronoun, which depends for its reference on nonlinguistic information outside the discourse context.

Beliavsky (1994) investigated the development of cohesive and noncohesive pronominal reference in the narratives of children in five age groups, kindergartners through fourth graders, and one group of adults. The subjects were given a book of pictures depicting a series of events and asked to tell the experimenter a story to fit the pictures. It was clear to them that the experimenter could not see the pictures. Beliavsky found three types of pronoun use. Associated with only the kindergarten children were pronouns whose referents were unrecoverable. These pronouns had no referent in the child's story; they referred to people or objects in the pictures accessible only to the child. Clearly, the presence of such pronouns detract from the cohesiveness of a narrative. Children of all ages, but none of the adults, used pronouns with ambiguous reference. Although the referent of the pronoun did appear in the child's narrative, there were two or more possible referents, and it was impossible to tell from the context which the child intended. All the adults and some of the children used cohesive pronouns, whose referent was uniquely recoverable from the narrative context. Because Beliavsky's study did not include children older than fourth grade, it is impossible to tell at what age ambiguous reference gives way to consistent fully cohesive use of pronouns.

In a study investigating 3- to 5-year-olds' ability to identify the referents of pronouns in story contexts, Umstead and Leonard (1983) found that referents within sentences were easier for the children to identify than were those in a previous sentence, even though the same number of words intervened between the referent and the pronoun in each case. There was no difference, however, between ease of identification of referents in the immediately preceding sentence and those in sentences three sentences back from the pronoun.

The ability to create cohesive, coherent texts, whether they be narratives or dialogues, is obviously essential to anyone's ability to communicate effectively with language. The ability to perceive the connectedness of texts is similarly essential for the comprehension of written material of all kinds and for the ability to read for information and pleasure.

The Development of Metalinguistic Skills

Most adults have the ability to do more with language than use it in communication. They are able to think about language as an object in its own right, to be aware of the form of language as separable from its content. For instance, if someone asks you whether "Himself was shaved by John" is a well-formed English sentence, you will be able to make the judgment that it is not, although you can understand what it means. Very young children seem not to be able to do this; nor can they make many other kinds of judgments that require the separation of the form of language from its content (de Villiers & de Villiers, 1972; Gleitman, Gleitman, & Shipley, 1972). Berthoud-Papandropoulou (1978) reported asking preschoolers for examples of short and long words. One child gave *train* as an example of a long word and *dandelion* as an example of a short one. The children could not separate the phonetic form of the words from the objects to which they refer. Similarly, Peters and Zaidel (1980) reported that, before the age of 4 1/2 children cannot identify words that sound alike but refer to different objects (e.g., *bat*). Only one fourth of the 3- and 4-year-olds studied by Tager-Flusberg and Smith (1980) could even reliably discriminate speech sounds from nonspeech sounds. There is a large literature documenting an explosion of metalinguistic abilities around early school age, including the ability to recognize ambiguous sentences, judge well-formedness, identify sentence pairs that are paraphrases of one another, and indicate awareness of the phonological structure of words. However, as mentioned in Chapter 3, a number of recent studies have demonstrated that children as young as 4, and even some 3-year-olds, given appropriate instruction and practice, can make a variety of judgments about the well-formedness and referential properties of sentences (Cairns, McDaniel, Hsu, & Rapp, 1994; McDaniel & Cairns, 1990; McDaniel, Chiu, & Maxfield, in press).

It has been widely believed (Hakes, 1980; Tunmer & Herriman, 1984; van Kleeck, 1982) that the ability to acquire metalinguistic skills is related to the child's entry into the concrete operational stage of cognitive development, as described by Piaget (Flavell, 1963). The work cited above casts doubt on that belief, however, since children typically do not achieve the stage of concrete operations until they are 5 or 6. Schlisselberg (1988; Schlisselberg & Cairns, 1995) conducted a study explicitly testing the relationship between cognitive development and metalinguistic skill. She measured children's ability to conserve, which is an important characteristic of concrete operational intelligence. Conservation is the ability to recognize that amounts of a solid or a liquid are the same even when their shape has been transformed—for example if liquid is poured from a tall, skinny glass into a short, wide one—or that the same number of objects are present whether or not they are arranged so that the line of one is longer than the line of another. Schlisselberg employed a number of measures of emerging conservation skill (developed by Gelman, 1982), as well as standard measures, and she employed the interview task described by McDaniel and Cairns (1990) to elicit judgments of well-formedness from children between the ages of 3 years, 5 months, and 6 years, 6 months. She found a high correlation between conservation ability and the ability to judge well-formedness. Furthermore, conservation ability was a better predictor of metalinguistic skill than was age. Thus, her study confirmed the belief that there is a relationship between cognitive development and metalinguistic skill. The question, however, is whether conservation ability is a prerequisite for metalinguistic skill. The answer seems to be no, as there were some children who achieved perfect scores on the well-formedness judgment task but who did not have perfect scores on the conservation test. On the other hand, there were no children who achieved perfect conservation scores who did not have perfect well-formedness scores. Thus, it appears that good metalinguistic skills may be a prerequisite for conservation skill, rather than the other way around.

Why might this be the case? Research by Donaldson and her colleagues (Donaldson, 1978; McGarrigle & Donaldson, 1974) suggests an answer. They proposed that a child must be able to deal with decontextualized language, with form divorced from content, if he is to score well on a conservation test. This is because the questions one asks children in standard conservation tests are pragmatically odd. For instance, the adult experimenter asks the child the same question twice about the quantity of liquid or solid material, after she herself has transformed it in some way. It is pragmatically odd to do this unless there is some reason to believe the quantity of material has changed. So the child is sort of tricked into saying it is now different. McGarrigle and Donaldson (1974) created an "accidental" transformation of the material and obtained more conserving responses from children 4 to 6 years of age than with the standard conservation test. Thus, the Donaldson hypothesis would predict exactly the kind of relationship between conservation score and well-formedness measure found by Schlisselberg (1988; Schlisselberg & Cairns, 1995).

How can we reconcile the common belief that metalinguistic skills do not develop until early school age and the finding that children in many experiments have exhibited the ability to make reliable well-formedness judgments? Perhaps the issue is spontaneity. Young children do not lack metalinguistic ability, but it must be elicited by specifically explaining what is required and giving them practice and feedback. Older children can get in touch with their metalinguistic skills with less explicit instruction. It is important to remember that the ability to use one's metalinguistic abilities varies greatly among adults and children, alike. The relationship between early reading ability and metalinguistic skill has been firmly established, but, like the relationship with cognitive development, the direction of causality is a puzzle. As we shall see below, it is almost certainly the case that some level of metalinguistic skill is necessary for the initial acquisition of reading ability, but learning to read also increases awareness of language. Now I turn to detailed consideration of a number of different aspects of metalinguistic skill: the ability to judge the well-formedness of sentences; the ability to judge pairs of sentences as synonymous; the ability to perceive the ambiguity of sentences; and the ability to perceive the phonological structure of words.

Some kinds of ill-formedness are easier for children to judge than others. Scrambled word order is typically the easiest kind of error for children to detect; in the Schlisselberg (1988) study mentioned above, sentences such as "*Ernie was going the slide down" were the easiest to judge and correct, whereas "*Where Cookie Monster was going?" and "*The woman pushed" were more difficult. Recall from Chapter 3 that McDaniel and Cairns and their colleagues have also elicited a slightly different kind of grammaticality judgment from their subjects. A sentence such as "Bert hit himself" is well formed on one meaning (i.e., that Bert is hitting himself) but ill formed on the meaning that Bert is hitting someone else. Children can be trained to make such judgments.

A number of studies have investigated the relationship between the ability to discriminate ill-formed and well-formed sentences and reading ability. Menyuk and Flood (cited in Menyuk, 1981) demonstrated a relationship between reading skill and metalinguistic abilities (including well-formedness judgments) from fourth graders to adults. More relevant to our understanding of the relationship between metalinguistic skill and early reading is Gindes's (1980) report that the ability to identify and explain ill-formed sentences is related to reading improvement scores a year later; her subjects were 4, 5, 6, and 7 years of age at the time of initial testing. In another study of very young children, Scholl and Ryan (1980) showed a strong correlation between the reading readiness scores of kindergarten children and their ability to judge the well-formedness of sentences. These children were prereaders, so it could not be the case that reading experience improved their metalinguistic abilities. Instead, the metalinguistic ability was related to other indicators of the children's preparedness for reading. The correlation coefficient in that study was .85, which is extremely high and indicates a very strong positive relationship between reading readiness scores and the judgment measure. Tunmer, Nesdale, and Wright (1987) compared good, younger readers with poor, older readers and found that the good readers scored significantly better than the poor readers on two measures of syntactic awareness. In a major 2-year longitudinal study of 118 first- and second-grade students, Tunmer, Herriman, and Nesdale (1988) demonstrated that both phonological awareness (measured by a syllable tapping task) and syntactic awareness (measured by a test of ability to correct sentences with scrambled word order) were significant predictors of subsequent reading ability. They concluded with the practical suggestion that schools provide preliterate children with intensive training in metalinguistic skills (using a variety of language games) before beginning reading instruction.

Two sentences are said to be synonymous, or paraphrases of one another, if they mean the same thing. A sentence is ambiguous if it has two (or more) meanings. Thus, ambiguity and paraphrase are essentially mirror images of one another. The ability to perceive paraphrase or ambiguity is based upon the realization that form and content can vary independently. Paraphrase occurs when two sentences with different forms have the same meaning; ambiguity occurs when a single form can carry more than one meaning. The ability to judge paraphrase and ambiguity, then, is a fundamental metalinguistic skill.

Beilin (1975) was the first to document that children can understand both the active and passive versions of a sentence without being able to report, given both versions simultaneously, that they mean the same thing. In the Hakes (1980) study, 6-year-old subjects could discriminate pairs of sentences that mean the same thing from pairs that do not, but the ability varied depending on the difficulty of the sentences involved. Easiest was the synonymous pair "There is an apple on the table" and "An apple is on the table," whereas the most difficult was "The nurse was called by the doctor" and "It was the nurse the doctor called." The ability to identify that two sentences are paraphrases of one another is probably the least studied of the metalinguistic skills.

Turning to studies of ambiguity detection, Peters and Zaidel (1980) tested the ability of children between the ages of 3 years, 3 months, and 6 years, 3 months, to identify two items that "have the same sound." They were shown panels of four pictures, two of which were homonyms, such as a baseball bat and a flying bat. Pretesting had ensured that the children knew all the words. Children below the age of 4 years, 4 months, were unable to identify the homonyms on the vast majority of the trials. The authors reported that the younger children clearly understood the task, and each child got at least one picture pair correct. They simply could not perceive that two words referring to different things sound the same. Although Peters and Zaidel reported a clear increase in scores for children above the age of 4 years, 4 months, even the oldest group did not achieve perfect scores.

Apparently the ability to judge the ambiguity of a sentence that turns on lexical homonymy is even more difficult than Peters and Zaidel's task. Wankoff (1983; Wankoff & Cairns, 1983) presented children from kindergarten through third grade with lexically ambiguous sentences such as "We saw the bat lying by the fence." The child was first asked if the sentence could mean more than one thing. If he said "no," there was a verbal prompt to elicit perception of the ambiguity. If the verbal prompt did not work, the child was shown two pictures depicting the two meanings of the ambiguity; in the example above, there would be a picture of a baseball bat lying by a fence and another of a flying rodent lying by a fence. The sentence was then repeated, and the child was once again asked if it could have two meanings. One would think that, by showing the children the pictures, Wankoff was giving away the ambiguity, but the results were quite dramatic. The kindergarten children almost never perceived the ambiguity of the sentences, and the first graders did so less than half the time. The second and third graders got almost all of them right, the difference being that the second graders needed the prompts more than the third graders did. Performance was much worse on structural ambiguities, sentences in which the two meanings depend on different structural analyses of unambiguous words. For instance, "The police were asked to stop smoking on the train" can mean either that the police were themselves smoking or that they were to stop someone else from smoking. Even with picture prompts the third graders perceived barely half of the structural ambiguities, and all the other children, including the second graders, did much worse. There was a significant correlation between ambiguity judgment ability and scores on a conservation test, with a much higher correlation of conservation ability with lexical ambiguity detection than with structural ambiguity detection. Shultz and Pilon (1973) also found that lexical ambiguities were easier to detect than structural ambiguities. They had subjects as old as 15 years who only detected 50% of the structural ambiguities in that study. There is no reason to believe that adults would perform differently from 15-year-olds. Structural ambiguities are more difficult to perceive than lexical ambiguities for people of every age.

Hirsh-Pasek, Gleitman, and Gleitman (1978) investigated ambiguity detection in children from Grades 1 through 6 in a very clever way. They presented children with jokes that turned on ambiguities of various sorts and asked the children to judge the humor of the jokes and explain why they were funny. There was a pronounced age effect, with the older children doing much better than the younger ones. The easiest jokes to "get" for everyone were those that hinged on a lexical ambiguity, such as "How do we know there was fruit on Noah's ark? Because the animals came in pairs." This fits with the experience of anyone who has spent time with children; they become great punsters in the early school years. Jokes that turned on structural ambiguity were appreciated less often by everyone, especially the younger children. An example is "Where would you go to see a man-eating fish? A seafood restaurant."

Both the Wankoff and Hirsh-Pasek et al. studies found a relationship between reading ability and ambiguity perception. Wankoff (1983; Wankoff & Cairns, 1983) demonstrated a strong relationship in her group of kindergarten through third-grade subjects between ambiguity perception and reading ability by a number of statistical tests relating the metalinguistic skill to a variety of reading measures. There were significant relationships between the ability to detect both lexical and structural ambiguities and all the reading measures: letter and word identification, word attack, and word and passage comprehension (subtests of the *Woodcock Reading Mastery* test). The strongest correlation was between passage comprehension and lexical ambiguity detection, with a correlation coefficient of .78. This indicates that these two abilities are closely linked. In the Hirsh-Pasek et al. (1978) study (Grades 1 through 6), there was a group of good and a group of poor readers. The groups were identified by the reading specialist at the school the children attended, and the authors pointed out that the poor readers were not truly disabled readers; they were simply having problems relative to the good readers at the upper middle class school that they attended. There was a highly significant effect of reading group on every type of ambiguity Hirsh-Pasek et al. investigated. They wrote that the poor readers performed consistently at a level about a year behind the good readers. For most of the ambiguity types, the difference between good and poor readers was more pronounced for the younger children.

In Chapter 4, I reviewed an on-line study of children's pronominal reference assignment (McKee, Nichol, & McDaniel, 1993). Another study (Swinney & Prather, 1990) used the same cross-modal priming task to investigate children's on-line processing of ambiguous words in sentences. Similar studies with adults (Swinney, 1979) had shown that when an ambiguous word is initially encountered, both of its meanings are accessed, even if there is prior sentential context biasing toward one of its meanings. This was an important demonstration of the modularity of the language processor from general cognition. A slightly later (but still on-line) process selects between possible meanings, directed by context. Swinney and Prather had two groups of subjects, one ages 4 years to 4 years, 7 months; the other, 4 years, 8 months, to 5 years, 6 months. The older group performed like adults, retrieving both meanings of the ambiguous words, regardless of context. The younger group, however, initially retrieved only the most frequent meaning of the ambiguous words, even if context biased them toward the least frequent. Swinney and Prather suggested that it may simply be the case that the least frequent meaning is retrieved more slowly by the younger children. In any event, their older group is about the same age (or a bit younger) than Wankoff's youngest subjects. Thus, it appears that the on-line processing of ambiguous words and sentences precedes a child's ability to consciously judge them as ambiguous. This is exactly what we would expect, as metalinguistic skills apparently develop later than the basic ability to produce and understand sentences.

Another interesting dissociation between the ability to use speech and the ability to make metalinguistic judgments about its structure is illustrated by research in the perception of the phonemic and syllabic properties of speech. I have mentioned a number of times in this book that the speech stream is continuous. There are no spaces between the words or between the individual speech sounds. Because of the phenomenon of coarticulation, at any given moment the articulators are affected by several different phonemes, and the acoustic signal reflects this. It is actually very interesting that we can perceptually segment this continuous physical signal into discrete words and speech sounds (i.e., phonemes). For instance, we perceive the word *cat* as being made up of the phoneme /k/ followed by /æ/ followed by /t/, although if we were to look at a spectrographic representation of the word we would see there is no physical segmentation of those sounds. Similarly, we can perceptually break up words into syllables. We know that the word *beautiful* consists of three syllables, although the entire word is a continuous sound. The ability to perceptually segment words into syllables and phonemes is an important metalinguistic skill that has been studied extensively by Liberman and her colleagues (Liberman, Shankweiler, Fischer, & Carter, 1974). Their technique is to train children to tap out either the syllables or the phonemes of a word. Thus, in the syllable-tapping task, the child is trained to tap once for *but*, twice for *butter*, and three times for *butter-fly*. In the phoneme-tapping task, the child is trained to tap once for the phoneme /u/, twice for *boo*, and three times for *boot*. It turns out that children of 4 can be taught the syllable segmentation task, but only children over the age of 6 can learn the phoneme segmentation task. This suggests that it is not until around the age of 6 that the child is able to perceive the speech signal as an ordered sequence of phonemes. Liberman, Shankweiler, Liberman, Fowler, and Fischer (1977) demonstrated that this ability not only is the result of reading instruction, but is a predictor of early reading success. They conducted the segmentation test with a group of first-grade children at the beginning of the school year (before reading instruction began) and demonstrated a relationship between their segmentation ability at the beginning of the year and their reading scores at the end of the year. Thus, the metalinguistic skill of segmentation is a significant predictor of reading success. (See Liberman & Shankweiler, 1985, for an excellent review of relevant literature.)

A summary of metalinguistic skills to this point suggests that the ability to judge well-formedness precedes the ability to judge paraphrases and sentential ambiguity and syllable segmentation precedes phoneme segmentation. The early school years are a period of rapid increase in metalinguistic skills of all types. Most important, these skills are highly related to reading readiness, reading improvement, reading acquisition in the early years, and reading skill in older children. I return to a discussion of this relationship after an examination of the reading process in general.

Reading

Although spoken language is biologically based, reading is purely a cultural phenomenon. The first writing system was developed over 5,000 years ago in Southern Mesopotamia (which is now Iraq). This was, of course, long after human evolution was complete and human languages were well established. A few writing systems (e.g., Chinese) consist of abstract characters corresponding to individual words, but the vast majority are composed of characters corresponding to units of spoken language, either syllables or, as in English, phonemes. Writing systems of the latter type are called alphabetic systems, and the match between the letter and the sound is called grapheme–phoneme correspondence.

The invention of alphabetic writing was a major accomplishment of human intelligence. The person who did it recognized, for the first time, that the metalinguistic perception of the continuous speech signal as a sequence of phonemes could be related to symbols that correspond to those perceptions. Everyone who learns to read an alphabetic system must replicate that experience in order to master grapheme–phoneme correspondences. Alphabetic systems vary in the quality of grapheme–phoneme correspondence. In German, for instance, it is almost perfect, but in English it is not. We have pronunciation oddities such as *ough* being pronounced differently in *cough*, *through*, and *dough*. Despite such notable exceptions, most of the words in English can be "sounded out" if one doesn't know them, and there are numerous spelling and pronunciation rules, such as an *–e* at the end of a word makes the vowel say its name (e.g., *hat* vs. *hate*), that work well most of the time.

Closely related to the fact that spoken language is biologically based and written language is purely cultural is another profound difference between the two. Every child growing up in a linguistic environment will naturally acquire the language of the environment, without needing to be taught. It is considered pathological if this does not happen in the normal course of maturation. This is, however, not the case with reading. Although some children whose parents read to them a lot do "teach themselves to read," this experience is extremely rare, even among very bright children. People must be taught to read; it does not develop as a result of maturation. Many adults of normal intelligence in the United States are nonliterate simply because they had to drop out of school at an early age, and there are many people in other parts of the world who are not literate because their language is not written. Thus, humans are not specially prepared to acquire the ability to read as they are to acquire the ability to produce and understand spoken language.

Think for a moment about some of the similarities and differences between reading a passage of text and carrying on a conversation. A fundamental difference is that when you hear speech it fades instantly, so processing (the conversion of sound to meaning) must be very rapid. In reading, the print is there permanently, so you can go back and reread something if necessary. There are spaces between the words, so a major segmentation problem is solved in reading. On the other hand, written language is decontextualized in a way that spoken language is not. There are fewer nonverbal or situational cues to aid in the derivation of meaning.

Although there are profound differences between reading and hearing, there are also profound similarities. Writing is parasitic on speech (Catts & Kamhi, 1987; Mattingly, 1972; Tunmer & Cole, 1985). Every morphological and syntactic element in spoken language is represented in written language, and each must be decoded from the printed page in order to derive the meaning of the written sentence. To understand the written sentence "The little girl hugged the kitty the puppy scared," you must represent the *–ed* of *hugged* and *scared* as a past tense morpheme, and you must unravel the relative clause to know which animal scared which. The meaning of a written sentence, like a spoken one, depends on its words and the structural relationships among them.

Thus, as words are read, they must be retrieved from one's internal lexicon, and one's knowledge of syntax must be employed to figure out the structure of the sentence, which determines its meaning. In fact, because written language is usually more precise than spoken language, it typically employs more complex syntactic structures than does conversational speech. Syntax tends to be quite complex in places where space is at a premium, such as newspapers.

When we say that the written language is parasitic on the spoken one, we mean that the same grammar and lexicon underlies comprehension of written and spoken sentences, and the same language processing routines must be applied to written sentences in order to compute a representation of their syntactic structure. Written language by its very nature constitutes the objectification of all elements of spoken language—phonemes, words, bound morphemes, and syntactic structure. It is clear, then, why metalinguistic skill and reading ability are so highly related. People who use only spoken language to communicate have no need to consider language as an object, distinct from the meaning it conveys. People who read must be able to do that, however, because the objectified language form is literally represented on the printed page. The correspondences between those written representations and the representations given by the internalized linguistic system must be discovered or the reading enterprise will fail. The greater the metalinguistic skill a person brings to the activity of learning to read, the easier it will be to make the appropriate connections.

The first connection, the one that gets the child "into" the system, is the grapheme–phoneme connection. We call this "cracking the code." But to make grapheme–phoneme connections, it is essential that one first be able to perceive both graphemes and phonemes. The letters are easy—they are laid out on the page in sequence; but the phonemes are buried inside a continuously varying speech signal. No wonder Liberman et al. (1977) demonstrated that the better a youngster's ability to perceive those phonemes, the more successful he will be at cracking the code. The first reading books employ conventional grapheme–phoneme mapping (no *cough* and *dough* at the beginning of first grade), very simple syntax, and uncomplicated narrative structures. At first the child's primary task is to crack the code and get into the system. As reading becomes more skilled, irregularly spelled words are introduced, the syntactic complexity of sentences increases, and texts become more structured. Cohesive linguistic devices must be recognized and properly interpreted, an activity that sometimes requires fairly complex inferential skills. The decontextualized written language must be interpreted based almost entirely on information appearing on the page. It is not surprising that these later reading abilities are highly related to the metalinguistic skills of well-formedness judgment and ambiguity detection. All require the ability to be aware of language as an object, separable from its meaning, but simultaneously to derive meaning from it.

Now let us move away from metalinguistic skills and examine the relationship between reading ability and the ordinary language abilities of speaking and understanding speech. This research typically contrasts the linguistic abilities of children who are good and poor readers. Because we know that reading is a skill that is parasitic on spoken language ability, we would expect children with more mature grammars and language *processing* skills to be more proficient early readers. In fact, children who are language impaired almost inevitably have difficulties in learning to read. Bishop and Edmondson (1987) reported a common phenomenon, whereby a child will have a language problem early, appear to catch up around the age of 5, then have difficulty with reading in first grade. Tallal (in an interview by Blakeslee, 1994) reported that 85% of children who are having difficulty with language acquisition by the age of 3 or 4 have difficulty reading later on in the school years. She and her colleagues (Curtiss, Katz, & Tallal, 1992) proposed a theory that a neurological deficiency in the temporal processing of rapidly presented information underlies both language and reading disabilities. Numerous studies have demonstrated language deficits in dyslexic children (Bowey & Patel, 1988; Butler, Marsh, Sheppard, & Sheppard, 1985; Catts, 1989; Scarborough, 1990; Vellutino, 1987). In an important longitudinal study of children 30 to 60 months of age, Scarborough (1991) demonstrated that the expressive and receptive syntactic skills of children destined to be dyslexic were significantly inferior to those of children who were destined to be skilled readers. Because children who are known to be language impaired are destined to have reading difficulties, it is reasonable to ask whether children who are having reading difficulties, but who have not been diagnosed as language impaired, might have subtle, unrecognized language difficulties. This possibility is reinforced by the observation that children with language disorders often appear to catch up with normally developing children by the age of 5, but then go on to have reading difficulties. Scarborough and Dobrich (1990) suggested that the appearance of catching up could be spurious, based on inadequate measurement of later language abilities. Therefore, there have been many studies comparing the language abilities of good and poor readers who have not been previously identified as having language problems.

Poor readers perform more poorly than do good readers on many language-specific tasks. For instance, poor readers are worse than good readers at identifying speech masked by noise, but are equivalent in their perception of nonlinguistic sounds (Brady, Shankweiler, & Mann, 1983). They are worse than good readers in memory of linguistic objects, such as words, letters, and nonsense words, but not in memory for unfamiliar faces and nonsense drawings (Liberman, Mann, Shankweiler, & Werfelman, 1982). Beyond the acknowledgment that language difficulties underlie reading deficits, a great deal of research has been designed to identify exactly what aspects of language processing are implicated. It has been amply demonstrated that poor readers perform worse than good readers on a wide variety of tasks related to phonological processing, decoding of nonsense words, and short-term memory for linguistic material that must be retained in its phonetic form (Mann, 1984, 1986). A particularly impressive demonstration of differences in phonetic short-term memory between good and poor readers comes from Mann, Liberman, and Shankweiler (1980; Mann & Liberman, 1984). They showed that in a short-term memory task good readers' memory for rhyming words is much worse than for nonrhyming ones, but this was not the case for poor readers. The explanation is that good readers' superior representation of the phonetic structure of the words in short-term memory gave rise to greater interference among the rhyming words for them relative to the poor readers.

A number of researchers have found poor readers to be deficient in either syntactic competence or in syntactic processing ability (Bentin, Deutsch, & Liberman, 1990; Byrne, 1981; Mann, 1984; Stein, Cairns, & Zurif, 1985; Vellutino, 1979). Many psycholinguists hold the view that children with reading impairments have difficulty in creating a syntactic representation of sentences. If this were true it would explain why some children are good decoders, but still have difficulty reading. This position has been challenged in a variety of studies demonstrating that the performance of poor readers on syntactic tasks can be improved with alterations of the experimental methodology to lighten memory load (Crain, 1987; Crain, Shankweiler, Macaruso, & Bar-Shalom, 1990), that the patterns of performance of good and poor readers on various syntactic constructions are similar (Smith, Macaruso, Shankweiler, & Crain, 1989), and that only those constructions that specifically tax short-term memory will elicit inferior performance from poor readers (Smith, Mann, & Shankweiler, 1986).

Shankweiler, Crain, Brady, and Macaruso (1992) articulated and reviewed evidence for their *processing limitation hypothesis* (the PLH). This theory identifies impaired phonological short-term memory as being responsible both for the reading difficulties and the apparent syntactic deficits of poor readers. For successful reading to take place, phonologically coded material must progress rapidly through the lexical, syntactic, and semantic processing systems. According to the PLH, the low-level deficit in processing phonological information creates a bottleneck that impedes the transfer of information to higher levels in the system. It is this inefficient transfer of information beginning at the lowest processing level that impairs higher level processing, whether it is manifested in reading difficulty or in impaired processing of syntactic constructions under conditions of excessive memory load. A massive study reported by Shankweiler and Katz

(1994), comparing good and poor readers, examined 353 children, ages 7 years, 5 months, to 9 years, 5 months. Their study provided impressive confirmation of the PLH. They found large differences in performance on tasks that directly tap phonological processes, such as phoneme segmentation, repetition of sequences of words and digits, and sentence repetition. However, they found virtually no difference in the groups' ability to match pictures with sentences of a variety of syntactic constructions.

Waltzman (1994; Waltzman & Cairns, 1995) investigated in a group of third graders two aspects of syntax that had never before been addressed in studies of the syntactic abilities of good and poor readers. In a judgment task using pictures to depict all possible interpretations of a variety of sentences, she evaluated the children's grammars with respect to all three of the binding principles (instantiated in both simple and complex structures), and the control principles as manifested in both infinitival complements and adverbial clauses (both of which I discussed in some detail in Chapter 3). The only syntactic characteristic that differentiated the two groups was obedience to Principle B of the binding theory. As we learned, Principle B is notorious for presenting difficulties for many children until late childhood. The reason is a mystery, but there is general agreement that whatever the problem is, it has to do with the child's developing principles of reference, and not with syntactic representations. Recall from the discussion in Chapter 4 that Grodzinsky and Reinhart (1993) have even suggested that short-term memory limitations may play a role in the Principle B problem. Waltzman also administered two measures of phonological short-term memory. While those scores did not correlate with the subjects' reading ability, they did show a significant relationship to total grammar score (which, of course, included Principle B performance). Waltzman's findings, then, support Shankweiler et al.'s (1992) PLH in that they do not demonstrate a purely syntactic deficit in the poor readers, but contradict it in that there was no relationship between short-term memory and reading skill. Furthermore, the discovery that poor readers are more likely than good readers to disobey Principle B opens up the possibility of yet another difference between good and poor readers, distinct from either phonological processing or basic syntactic ability.

There seems, then, to be a conflict between the studies that indicate that dyslexic children have inferior language skills across the board, including syntactic as well as phonological difficulties, and studies indicating that good and poor readers have only a problem in representing phonological material in short-term memory. It is possible that the distinction here is in severity of reading impairment. Children who have a language impairment that extends to syntactic and phonological processing will have a more profound reading disability than children with intact syntax and phonological problems alone. The relationship between metalinguistic skills and reading ability, however, seems much more profound. Differences among early readers can be predicted by their metalinguistic skills even if the reading difficulties are not sufficiently severe to classify them as dyslexic. This interpretation, while plausible, is speculative. Studies of language and reading vary widely in the measures of reading ability employed, the aspects of language investigated, and the general setup of the studies. What we can say with certainty, however, is that the fields of developmental psycholinguistics, reading, and speech–language pathology must work closely together if progress is to be made in the theoretical understanding of early reading and the application of that understanding to the diagnosis and remediation of reading difficulties.

Epilogue

In this book I have intended to depict first language acquisition as the result of a rich interaction between biological, inborn properties of the developing child and her experience with language. I hope that the reader comes away with a sense that the field of language acquisition is coherent, dynamic, healthy, and—most important of all—very exciting.

References

Allen, G. D., & Hawkins, S. (1980). Phonological rhythm: Definition and development. In G. H. Yeni-Komshian, J.F. Kavanagh, & C. A. Ferguson (Eds.), *Child phonology: Vol. 1. Production.* New York: Academic Press.

Anderson, A. H., Clark, A., & Mullin, J. (1991). Introducing information in dialogues: Forms of introduction chosen by young speakers and the responses elicited from young listeners. *Journal of Child Language, 18,* 663–687.

Anderson, A. H., Clark, A., & Mullin, J. (1994). Interactive communication between children: Learning how to make language work in dialogue. *Journal of Child Language, 21,* 439–464.

Anderson, E. W. (1978). Will you don't snore please? Directives in young children's role-play speech. *Papers and Reports on Child Language Development, 15,* 140–150.

Atkinson, M. (1992). *Children's syntax: An introduction to Principles and Parameters theory.* Oxford: Blackwell.

Austin, J. L. (1962). *How to do things with words.* Oxford: Oxford University Press.

Baillargeon, R. (1987). Object permanence in 3.5- and 4.5-month-old infants. *Developmental Psychology, 23,* 655–664.

Baker, C. L. (1979). Syntactic theory and the projection problem. *Linguistic Inquiry, 12,* 533–581.

Baldwin, D. A. (1991). Infant contributions to the achievement of joint reference. *Child Development, 62.* Reprinted in P. Bloom (Ed.), (1994), *Language acquisition: Core readings* (pp. 129–153). Cambridge, MA: MIT Press.

Bates, E., Camioni, L., & Volterra, V. (1979). The acquisition of performatives prior to speech. In E. Ochs & B. Schiefflin (Eds.), *Developmental pragmatics*. New York: Academic Press.

Bates, E., Marchman, V., Thal, D., Fenson, L., Dale, P., Reznick, J. S., Reilly, J., & Hartung, J. (1994). Developmental and stylistic variation in the composition of early vocabulary. *Journal of Child Language, 21*, 85–124.

Beilin, H. (1975). *Studies in the cognitive basis of language development*. New York: Academic Press.

Beliavsky, N. (1994). *The evolution of pronominal reference in children's narratives: Who are "they"?* Unpublished doctoral dissertation, Northwestern University, Evanston, IL.

Benedict, H. (1979). Early lexical development: Comprehension and production. *Journal of Child Language, 6*, 183–200.

Bentin, S., Deutsch, A., & Liberman, I. Y. (1990). Syntactic competence and reading ability in children. *Journal of Exceptional Child Psychology, 49*, 147–172.

Berthoud-Papandropoulou, I. (1978). An experimental study of children's ideas about language. In A. Sinclair, R. J. Jarvella, & W. J. M. Levelt (Eds.), *The child's conception of language* (pp. 55–64). Berlin: Springer.

Bickerton, D. (1984). The language bioprogram hypothesis. *The Behavioral and Brain Sciences, 7*(2), 173–221.

Bickerton, D. (1988). Creole languages and the bioprogram. In F. J. Newmeyer (Ed.), *Linguistics: The Cambridge Survey. Vol. 2: Linguistic theory: Extensions and implications* (pp. 268–284). Cambridge, England: Cambridge University Press.

Bishop, D. V. M., & Edmondson, A. (1987). Language-impaired 4-year-olds: Distinguishing transient from persistent impairment. *Journal of Speech and Hearing Disorders, 52*, 156–173.

Blakeslee, S. (1994, August 16). New clue to cause of dyslexia seen in mishearing of fast sounds. *New York Times*, p. C1.

Bloom, L. (1970). *Language development: Form and function in emerging grammars*. Cambridge, MA: MIT Press.

Bloom, L., & Lahey, M. (1978). *Language development and language disorders*. New York: Wiley.

Bloom, L., Lahey, M., Hood, L., Lifter, K., & Fiess, K. (1980). Complex sentences: Acquisition of syntactic connectives and the semantic relations they encode. *Journal of Child Language, 7*, 235–262.

Bloom, L., Rocissano, L., & Hood, L. (1976). Adult–child discourse: Developmental interaction between information processing and linguistic knowledge. *Cognitive Psychology, 8*, 521–552.

Bloom, L., Tackeff, J., & Lahey, M. (1984). Learning *to* in complement constructions. *Journal of Child Language, 11*, 391-406.

Bloom, P. (1990). Subjectless sentences in child language. *Linguistic Inquiry, 21*, 491–504.

Bloom, P., Barss, A., Nicol, J., & Conway, L. (1994). Children's knowledge of binding and coreference: Evidence from spontaneous speech. *Language, 70*, 53–71.

Bloomfield, L. (1933). *Language*. New York: Holt, Rinehart & Winston.

Blumenthal, A. L. (1967). Prompted recall of sentences. *Journal of Verbal Learning and Verbal Behavior, 6*, 674–676.

Bowey, J. A., & Patel, R. K. (1988). Metalinguistic ability and early reading achievement. *Applied Psycholinguistics, 1*, 367–383.

Boysson-Bardies, B. de, Sagart, L., & Durand, C. (1984). Discernible differences in the babbling of infants according to target language. *Journal of Child Language, 11*, 1–15.

Brady, S., Shankweiler, D., & Mann, V. A. (1983). Speech perception and memory code in relation to reading ability. *Journal of Experimental Child Psychology, 34*, 345–367.

Braine, M. (1973). Three suggestions regarding grammatical analyses of children's language. In C. Ferguson & D. Slobin (Eds.), *Studies in child language development*. New York: Holt, Rinehart & Winston.

Brown, G., & Yule, G. (1983). *Discourse analysis*. Cambridge, England: Cambridge University Press.

Brown, R. (1957). Linguistic determinism and the parts of speech. *Journal of Abnormal and Social Psychology, 55*, 1–5.

Brown, R. (1973). *A first language*. Cambridge, MA: Harvard University Press.

Brown, R., & Hanlon, C. (1970). Derivational complexity and order of acquisition in child speech. In J. R. Hayes (Ed.), *Cognition and the development of language* (pp. 11–54). New York: Wiley.

Butler, S. R., Marsh, H. W., Sheppard, M. J., & Sheppard, J. L. (1985). Seven-year longitudinal study of the early prediction of reading achievement. *Journal of Educational Psychology, 77*, 349–361.

Byrne, B. (1981). Deficient syntactic control in poor readers: Is a weak phonetic memory code responsible? *Applied Psycholinguistics, 2*, 201–212.

Cairns, H. S. (1991). Not in the absence of experience. Commentary on Crain, S. Language acquisition in the absence of experience. *Behavioral and Brain Sciences, 14*, 614–615.

Cairns, H. S., & Cairns, C. E. (1976). *Psycholinguistics: A cognitive view of language*. New York: Holt, Rinehart & Winston.

Cairns, H. S., Cairns, C. E., & Williams, F. (1974). Some theoretical considerations of articulation substitution phenomena. *Language and Speech, 17*, 160–173.

Cairns, H. S., & McDaniel, D. (1991). The notion of "innateness" in language acquisition: Some empirical consequences. *CUNY Forum, 16*, 19–37.

Cairns, H. S., McDaniel, D., Hsu, J. R., Parsons, S., & Konstantyn, D. (1994, January). *The pronoun coreference requirement: Grammar or pragmatics?* Paper presented at the Boston University Child Language Conference, Boston.

Cairns, H. S., McDaniel, D., Hsu, J. R., DeFino, S., & Konstantyn, D. (in press). Grammatical and discourse principles in children's grammars: The pronoun coreference requirement. *CUNY Forum.*

Cairns, H. S., McDaniel, D., Hsu, J. R., & Rapp, M. (1994). A longitudinal study of principles of control and pronominal reference in child English. *Language, 70,* 260–288.

Carey, S. (1978). The child as word learner. In M. Halle, J. Bresnan, & G. A. Miller (Eds.), *Linguistic theory and psychological reality* (pp. 264–293). Cambridge, MA: MIT Press.

Carey, S. (1982). Semantic development: The state of the art. In E. Wanner & L. R. Gleitman (Eds.), *Language acquisition: The state of the art* (pp. 347–389). Cambridge, England: Cambridge University Press.

Catts, H. W. (1989). Defining dyslexia as a developmental language disorder. *Annals of Dyslexia, 39,* 50–64.

Catts, H. W., & Kamhi, A. G. (1987). Relationship between reading and language disorders: Implications for the speech–language pathologist. *Seminars in Speech and Language, 8,* 377–392.

Cazden, C. B. (1965). *Environmental assistance to the child's acquisition of grammar.* Unpublished doctoral dissertation, Harvard University, Cambridge, MA.

Chapman, R. S., & Kohn, L. L. (1977, March). *Comprehension strategies in preschoolers: Animate agents or probable events?* Paper presented to Stanford Child Language Research Forum, Stanford University, Stanford, CA.

Chien, Y-C., & Wexler, K. (1990). Children's knowledge of locality conditions in binding as evidence for the modularity of syntax and pragmatics. *Language Acquisition: A Journal of Developmental Linguistics, 1,* 225–295.

Chomsky, C. (1969). *The acquisition of syntax in children from 5 to 10.* Cambridge, MA: MIT Press.

Chomsky, N. (1981). *Lectures on government and binding: The Pisa lectures.* Dordrecht: Foris Publications.

Clark, E. V. (1971). On the acquisition of the meaning of "before" and "after." *Journal of Verbal Learning and Verbal Behavior, 10,* 266–275.

Clark, E. V. (1972). On the child's acquisition of antonyms in two semantic fields. *Journal of Verbal Learning and Verbal Behavior, 11,* 750–758.

Clark, E. V. (1983). Meanings and concepts. In J. H. Flavell & E. M. Markman (Eds.), *Handbook of child psychology: Vol. 3. Cognitive development* (pp. 787–840). New York: Wiley.

Clark, E. V., & Garnica, 0. (1974). Is he coming or going? On the acquisition of deictic verbs. *Journal of Verbal Learning and Verbal Behavior, 13,* 559–573.

Clark, E. V., & Senegul, C. (1978). Strategies in the acquisition of deixis. *Journal of Child Language, 5,* 457–475.

Condron, W. S., & Sander, L. W. (1974). Synchrony demonstrated between movements of the neonate and adult speech. *Child Development, 65,* 456–462.

Connell, P. (1986). Teaching subjecthood to language-disordered children. *Journal of Speech and Hearing Research, 29,* 481–492.

Crain, S. (1987). On performability: Structure and process in language understanding. *Clinical Linguistics and Phonetics, 1,* 127–145.

Crain, S. (1991). Language acquisition in the absence of experience. *Behavioral and Brain Sciences, 14,* 597–650.

Crain, S., & McKee, C. (1985, November). *Children's adherence to structural restrictions on coreference.* Paper presented at the meeting of the Northeastern Linguistic Society, McGill University, Montreal.

Crain, S., McKee, C., & Emiliani, M. (1990). Visiting relatives in Italy. In L. Frazier & J. de Villiers (Eds.), *Language processing and language acquisition* (pp. 335–356). Boston: Kluwer.

Crain, S., & Nakayama, M. (1986). Structure dependence in children's language. *Language, 63,* 522–543.

Crain, S., Shankweiler, D., Macaruso, P., & Bar-Shalom, E. (1990). Working memory and comprehension of spoken sentences: Investigations of children with reading disorders. In G. Vallar & T. Shallice (Eds.), *Neuropsychological impairments of short-term memory* (pp. 477–508). Cambridge, England: Cambridge University Press.

Crain, S., Thornton, R., Boster, C., Conway, L., Lillo-Martin, D., & Woodams, E. (1995). *Quantification without qualification.* Manuscript in preparation.

Cromer, R. (1970). Children are nice to understand: Surface structure clues for the recovery of a deep structure. *British Journal of Psychology, 61,* 397–408.

Curtiss, S. (1977). *Genie: A psycholinguistic study of a modern-day "wild child."* New York: Academic Press.

Curtiss, S. (1988). Abnormal language acquisition and the modularity of language. In F. J. Newmeyer (Ed.), *Linguistics: The Cambridge Survey. Vol. 2. Linguistic theory: Extensions and implications* (pp. 96–116). Cambridge, England: Cambridge University Press.

Curtiss, S., Fromkin, V., Krashen, S., Rigler, D., & Rigler, M. (1974). The linguistic development of Genie. *Language, 50,* 528–554.

Curtiss, S., Katz, W., & Tallal, P. (1992). Delay versus deviance in the language acquisition of language-impaired children. *Journal of Speech and Hearing Research, 35,* 373–383.

Dawkins, M. S. (1986). *Unraveling animal behavior.* Essex: Longman.

Demetras, M. J., Post, K. N., & Snow, C. E. (1986). Feedback to first language learners: The role of repetitions and clarification questions. *Journal of Child Language, 13,* 275–292.

de Villiers, J., & de Villiers, P. (1973). A cross-sectional study of the development of grammatical morphemes in child speech. *Journal of Psycholinguistic Research, 2,* 267–268.

de Villiers, J., & de Villiers, P. (1974). On this, that, and the other: Nonegocentrism in very young children. *Journal of Experimental Child Psychology, 18,* 438–447.

de Villiers, J., & de Villiers, P. (1978). *Language acquisition.* Cambridge, MA: Harvard University Press.

de Villiers, J., & Roeper, T. (1990). Introduction: Acquisition of wh– movement. In T. L. Maxfield & B. Plunkett (Eds.), *University of Massachusetts Occasional Papers: Papers in the acquisition of WH* (pp. 118).

de Villiers, J., Roeper, T., & Vainikka, A. (1990). The acquisition of long-distance rules. In L. Frazier & J. de Villiers (Eds.), *Language processing and language acquisition* (pp. 257–298). Boston: Kluwer.

de Villiers, P., & de Villiers, J. (1972). Early judgments of semantic and syntactic acceptability by children. *Journal of Psycholinguistic Research, 1,* 299–310.

Donaldson, M. (1978). *Children's minds.* New York: Norton.

Donaldson, M., & Balfour, G. (1968). Less is more: A study of language comprehension in children. *British Journal of Psychology, 59,* 461–471.

Dore, J. (1974). A pragmatic description of early language development. *Journal of Psycholinguistic Research, 3,* 343–350.

Dore, J. (1977). Oh them sheriff: A pragmatic analysis of children's responses to questions. In S. Ervin-Tripp & C. Mitchell-Kernan (Eds.), *Child discourse.* New York: Academic Press.

Dore, J., Gearhart, M., & Newman, D. (1978). The structure of nursery school conversation. In K. Nelson (Ed.), *Children's language* (Vol. 1, pp. 337–395). New York: Gardner Press.

Dromi, E. (1987). *Early lexical development.* Cambridge, MA: Cambridge University Press.

Echols, C. H. (1992). *Developmental changes in attention to labeled events during the transition to language.* Paper presented at the International Conference for Infant Studies, Miami Beach, FL.

Eimas, P. D. (1975). Developmental studies in speech perception. In L. B. Cohen & P. Salapatek (Eds.), *Infant perception: From sensation to cognition* (Vol. 2, pp. 193–231).

Eisenberg, S. (1989). *The development of infinitives by three, four, and five year old children.* Unpublished doctoral dissertation, The City University of New York.

Eisenberg, S., & Cairns, H. S. (1994). The development of infinitives from three to five. *Journal of Child Language, 21,* 713–734.

Entus, A. K. (1975). *Hemisphere asymmetry in processing of dichotically presented speech and nonspeech stimuli by infants.* Paper presented at the biennial meeting of the Society for Research in Child Development, Denver.

Ervin-Tripp, S. (1977). Wait for me, roller skate. In S. Ervin-Tripp & C. Mitchell-Kernan (Eds.), *Child discourse*. New York: Academic Press.

Feldman, C. (1971). *The effects of various types of adult responses in the syntactic acquisition of two- to three-year-olds*. Unpublished manuscript, University of Chicago.

Fernald, A. (1992). Human maternal vocalizations to infants as biologically relevant signals: An evolutionary perspective. In Barkow et al., *The adapted mind: Evolutionary psychology and the generation of culture*. Oxford: Oxford University Press. Reprinted in P. Bloom (Ed.), (1994). *Language acquisition: Core readings* (pp. 51–94). Cambridge, MA: MIT Press.

Flavell, J. H. (1963). *The developmental psychology of Jean Piaget*. Princeton, NJ: D. Van Nostrand.

Fodor, J. A. (1975). *The language of thought*. New York: Crowell.

Fodor, J. A., & Bever, T. G. (1965). The psychological reality of linguistic segments. *Journal of Verbal Learning and Verbal Behavior, 4*, 414–420.

Fodor, J. D. (1985, October). *Why learn lexical rules?* Paper presented at the Tenth Annual Boston University Conference on Language Development. Written up as "The procedural solution to the projection problem," unpublished manuscript, The City University of New York.

Foss, D. J., & Hakes, D. T. (1978). *Psycholinguistics: An introduction to the psychology of language*. Englewood Cliffs, NJ: Prentice-Hall.

Foster, S. H. (1981). Interpreting child discourse. In P. French & M. MacLure (Eds.), *Adult–child conversation* (pp. 268–286). London: Croom Helm.

Foster, S. H. (1985, March). The development of discourse topic skills by infants and young children. *Topics in Language Disorders*, pp. 31–45.

Foster, S. H. (1986). Learning discourse topic management in the preschool years. *Journal of Child Language, 13*, 231–250.

Foster, S. H. (1990). *The communicative competence of young children*. New York: Longman.

Foster-Cohen, S. H. (1994). Exploring the boundary between syntax and pragmatics: Relevance and the binding of pronouns. *Journal of Child Language, 21*, 237–255.

Franks, S., & Connell, P. (in press). Knowledge of binding in normal and SLI children. *Journal of Child Language*.

Fremgen, A., & Fay, D. (1980). Overextensions in production and comprehension: A methodological clarification. *Journal of Child Language, 7*, 205–211.

Gallagher, T. M. (1991). *Pragmatics of language: Clinical practice issues*. San Diego, CA: Singular Publishing Group.

Garrett, M. F. (1988). Processes in language production. In F. J. Newnteyer (Ed.), *Linguistics: The Cambridge Survey. Vol. 3. Language: Psychological and biological aspects* (pp. 69–96). Cambridge, England: Cambridge University Press.

Garvey, C. (1975). Requests and responses in children's speech. *Journal of Child Language, 2*, 41–60.

Gelman, R. (1982). Accessing one-to-one correspondence: Still another paper about conservation. *British Journal of Psychology, 73*, 209–220.

Gentner, D. (1983). Why nouns are learned before verbs: Linguistic relativity versus natural partitioning. In S. Kuczaj (Ed.), *Language development: Vol. 2. Language, cognition, and culture*. Hillsdale, NJ: Erlbaum.

Gerken, L. A., & McIntosh, B. J. (1993). The interplay of function morphemes and prosody in early language. *Developmental Psychology, 29*, 448–457.

Gerken, L. A., & McIntosh, B. J. (1995). *Function morphemes in the sentence comprehension of normally developing and language delayed children*. Manuscript in preparation.

Gindes, M. (1980, April). *The development of metalinguistic knowledge and its relation to reading acquisition*. Paper presented at the Conference on the Language of the Young Child: Frontiers of Research, Brooklyn College, City University of New York.

Gleitman, L. (1990). The structural sources of verb meaning. *Language Acquisition: A Journal of Developmental Linguistics, 1*, 3–55. Reprinted in P. Bloom (Ed.), (1994), *Language acquisition: Core readings*. Cambridge, MA: MIT Press.

Gleitman, L. R., Gleitman, H., & Shipley, E. F. (1972). The emergence of the child as grammarian. *Cognition, 1*, 137–164.

Gleitman, L. R., Newport, E. L., & Gleitman, H. (1984). The current status of the motherese hypothesis. *Journal of Child Language, 11*, 43–79.

Gleitman, L. R., & Wanner, E. (1984). Richly specified input to language learning. In 0. Selfridge, E. L. Rissland, & M. Arbib (Eds.), *Adaptive control of ill-defined systems*. New York: Plenum.

Goldin-Meadow, S., & Mylander, C. (1990). Beyond the input given: The child's role in the acquisition of language. *Language, 66*, 2. Reprinted in P. Bloom (Ed.), (1994). *Language acquisition: Core readings* (pp. 507–542). Cambridge, MA: MIT Press.

Golinkoff, R. M. (1986). "I beg your pardon": The preverbal negotiation of failed messages. *Journal of Child Language, 13*, 455–476.

Golinkoff, R. M., Kenealy, L., & Hirsh-Pasek, K. (1993). *Object scope: Labels promote attention to whole objects*. Unpublished manuscript, University of Delaware, Newark.

Golinkoff, R. M., Mervis, C. B., & Hirsh-Pasek, K. (1994). Early object labels: The case for a developmental lexical principles framework. *Journal of Child Language, 21*, 125–156.

Goodluck, H. (1981). Children's grammar of complement–subject interpretation. In S. L. Tavakolian (Ed.), *Language acquisition and linguistic therapy* (pp. 139–166). Cambridge, MA: MIT Press.

Goodluck, H. (1987). Children's interpretations of pronouns and null NP's: An alternative view. In B. Lust (Ed.), *Studies in the acquisition of anaphora: Vol. 2. Applying the constraints* (pp. 247–269). Boston: Reidel.

Goodluck, H. (1988). Language acquisition and linguistic theory. In P. Fletcher & M. Garmon (Eds.), *Language acquisition* (2nd ed., pp. 49–68). Cambridge, England: Cambridge University Press.

Goodluck, H. (1991). *Language acquisition: A linguistic introduction.* Cambridge, MA: Blackwell.

Goodluck, H., & Tavakolian, S. L. (1982). Competence and processing in children's grammar of relative clauses. *Cognition, 11*, 1–27.

Gopnik, M. (1990). Feature blindness: A case study. *Language Acquisition: A Journal of Developmental Linguistics, 1*, 139–164.

Greenfield, P. M., & Smith, J. H. (1976). *The structure of communication in early language development.* New York: Academic Press.

Grodzinsky, Y., & Kave, G. (1993/1994). Do children really know condition A? *Language Acquisition: A Journal of Developmental Linguistics, 3*, 41–54.

Grodzinsky, Y., & Reinhart, T. (1993). The innateness of binding and coreference. *Linguistic Inquiry, 24*, 69–101.

Gropen, J., Pinker, S., Hollander, M., & Goldberg, R. (1991). *Cognition, 41.* Reprinted in P. Bloom (Ed.), (1994), *Language acquisition: Core readings* (pp. 285–328). Cambridge, MA: MIT Press.

Gropen, J., Pinker, S., Hollander, M., Goldberg, R., & Wilson, R. (1989). The learnability and acquisition of the dative alternation in English. *Language, 65*, 203–257.

Hakes, D. T. (1980). *The development of metalinguistic abilities in children.* New York: Springer.

Halliday, M. A. K. (1973). *Explorations in the functions of language.* London: Edward Arnold.

Halliday, M. A. K. (1975). *Learning how to mean: Explorations in the development of language.* London: Edward Arnold.

Halliday, M. A. K., & Hasan, R. (1976). *Cohesion in English.* New York: Longman.

Hamburger, H., & Crain, S. (1982). Relative acquisition. In S. A. Kuczaj II (Ed.), *Language development: Vol. I: Syntax and semantics* (pp. 245–274). Hillsdale, NJ: Erlbaum.

Hirsh-Pasek, K., Gleitman, L. R., & Gleitman, H. (1978). What did the brain say to the mind? A study of the detection and report of ambiguity by young children. In A. Sinclair, R. J. Jarvella, & J. M. Levelt (Eds.), *The child's conception of language* (pp. 97–132). Berlin: Springer.

Hirsh-Pasek, K., Nelson, D. G. N., Jusczyk, P. W., Cassidy, K. W., Druss, B., & Kennedy, L. (1987). Clauses are perceptual units for young infants. *Cognition, 26*, 269–286.

Hirsh-Pasek, K., Treiman, R., & Schneiderman, M. (1984). Brown and Hanlon revisited: Mother's sensitivity to ungrammatical forms. *Journal of Child Language, 11*, 81–88.

Hoff-Ginsburg, E., & Shatz, M. (1982). Linguistic input and the child's acquisition of language. *Psychological Bulletin, 92*, 3–26.

Horgan, D. (1978). The development of the full passive. *Journal of Child Language, 5*, 65–80.

Hsu, J. R. (1981). *The development of structural principles related to complement subject interpretation.* Unpublished doctoral dissertation, City University of New York.

Hsu, J. R., Cairns, H. S., Eisenberg, S., & Schlisselberg, G. (1989). Control and coreference in early child language. *Journal of Child Language, 16*, 599–622.

Hsu, J. R., Cairns, H. S., Eisenberg, S., & Schlisselberg, G. (1991). When do children avoid backwards coreference? *Journal of Child Language, 18*, 339–353.

Hsu, J. R., Cairns, H. S., & Fiengo, R. W. (1985). The development of grammars underlying children's interpretation of complex sentences. *Cognition, 20*, 25–48.

Hyams, N. (1984). The acquisition of infinitival complements: A reply to Bloom, Tackeff & Lahey. *Journal of Child Language, 11*, 679–683.

Hyams, N. M. (1986). *Language acquisition and the theory of parameters.* Boston: Reidel.

Hyams, N. (1994, March). *The underspecification of functional categories in early grammar.* Paper presented at the Great Britain Child Language Seminar, Bangor, Wales.

Ingham, R. (1993/1994). Input and learnability: Direct-object omissibility in English. *Language Acquisition: A Journal of Developmental Linguistics, 3*, 95–120.

Ingram, D. (1988). Phonological development: Production. In P. Fletcher & M. Garman (Eds.), *Language acquisition* (2nd ed., pp. 223–239). Cambridge, England: Cambridge University Press.

Ingram, D., Christensen, L., Veach, S., & Webster, B. (1980). The acquisition of word-initial fricatives and affricates in English by children between 2 and 6 years. In G. H. Yeni-Komshian, J. F. Davanagh, & C. A. Ferguson (Eds.), *Child phonology: Vol. 1. Production* (pp. 169–192). New York: Academic Press.

Ingram, D., & Shaw, C. (1981). *The comprehension of prenominal reference in children.* Unpublished manuscript, The University of British Columbia, Vancouver.

Inhelder, B., & Piaget, J. (1964). *The early growth of logic in the child.* London: Routledge and Kegan Paul.

Jarmulowicz, L. D. (1994). *Developmental evidence for an acquisition sequence of verbs with and without external arguments.* Unpublished manuscript, City University of New York.

Jusczyk, P. W., & Anslin, R. N. (in press). Infants' detection of the sound patterns of words in fluent speech. *Cognitive Psychology*.

Karmiloff-Smith, A. (1986). Some fundamental aspects of language development after the age of 5. In P. Fletcher & M. Garman (Eds.), *Language acquisition* (2nd ed.). Cambridge, England: Cambridge University Press.

Katz, N., Baker, E., & Macnamara, J. (1974). What's in a name? A study of how children learn common and proper names. *Child Development, 45*, 469–473.

Kess, J. F. (1992). *Psycholinguistics: Psychology, linguistics, and the study of natural language*. Philadelphia: John Benjamins.

Kewley-Port, D., & Preston, M. S. (1974). Early apical stop production: A voice onset time analysis. *Journal of Phonetics, 2*, 195–210.

King, M. L., & Rentel, V. M. (1981). *How children learn to write: A longitudinal study*. Final report to National Institute of Education, Columbus: Ohio State University. (ERIC Document Reproduction Service No. ED 213 050)

Klecan-Aker, J. S., & Lopez, B. (1985). A comparison of T-units and cohesive ties used by first grade children. *Language and Speech, 28*, 307–315.

Klima, E., & Bellugi, U. (1973). Syntactic regularities in the speech of children. In C. A. Ferguson & D. I. Slobin (Eds.), *Studies of child language development* (pp. 333–354). New York: Holt, Rinehart & Winston.

Klima, E., & Bellugi, U. (1979). *The signs of language*. Cambridge, MA: Harvard University Press.

Krauss, R. M., & Glucksberg, S. (1977, February). Social and non-social speech. *Scientific American*, pp. 100–105.

Kuczaj, S. A., & Maratsos, M. (1975). On the acquisition of "front," "back," and "side." *Child Development, 46*, 202–210.

Kuhl, P. (1992). Psychoacoustics and speech perception: Internal standards, perceptual anchors, and prototypes. In L. A. Werner & E. Rubel (Eds.), *Developmental psychoacoustics*. Washington, DC: American Psychological Association.

Kuhn, T. S. (1962). *The structure of scientific revolutions*. Chicago: University of Chicago Press.

Lenneberg, E. H. (1967). *Biological foundations of language*. Cambridge, MA: MIT Press.

Leonard, L. B. (1972). What is deviant language? *Journal of Speech and Hearing Disorders, 37*, 427–446.

Leonard, L. B. (1989). Language learnability and specific language impairment in children. *Applied Psycholinguistics, 10*, 179–202.

Leonard, L. B. (1992). Morphological deficits in children with specific language impairment: The status of features in the underlying grammar. *Language Acquisition: A Journal of Developmental Linguistics, 2*, 151–180.

Leonard, L. B. (1994). Language disorders in preschool children. In G. H. Shames, E. H. Wiig, & W. A. Secord (Eds.), *Human communication disorders: An introduction* (pp. 174–211). New York: Merrill.

Leonard, L. B. (1995). *Functional categories in the grammars of children with specific language impairment.* Manuscript in preparation.

Leonard, L. B., Bortolini, U., Caselli, M. C., McGregor, K. K., & Sabbadini, L. (1992). Morphological deficits in children with specific language impairment: The status of features in the underlying grammar. *Language Acquisition: A Journal of Developmental Linguistics, 2*, 151–180.

Leonard, L. B., Wilcox, M., Fulmer, K., & Dans, G. (1978). Understanding indirect requests: An investigation of children's comprehension of pragmatic meanings. *Journal of Speech and Hearing Research, 21*, 528–537.

Liberman, I. Y., Mann, V. A., Shankweiler, D., & Werfelman, M. (1982). Children's memory for recurring linguistic and non-linguistic material in relation to reading ability. *Cortex, 18*, 367–375.

Liberman, I. Y., & Shankweiler, D. (1985). Phonology and the problems of learning to read and write. *Remedial and Special Education, 6*, 8–17.

Liberman, I. Y., Shankweiler, D., Fischer, F. W., & Carter, B. (1974). Explicit syllable and phoneme segmentation in the young child. *Journal of Experimental Child Psychology, 18*, 201–212.

Liberman, I. Y., Shankweiler, D., Liberman, A. M., Fowler, C., & Fischer, F. W. (1977). Phonetic segmentation and recoding in the beginning reader. In A. S. Reber & D. L. Scarborough (Eds.), *Toward a psychology of reading* (pp. 207–226). Hillsdale, NJ: Erlbaum.

Lieberman, A. F., & Garvey, C. (1977). *Interpersonal pauses in preschoolers' verbal exchanges.* Paper presented at the Biennial Meeting of the Society for Research in Child Development, New Orleans.

Lieberman, P. (1980). On the development of vowel production in young children. In G. H. Yeni-Komshian, J. F. Davanagh, & C. A. Ferguson (Eds.), *Child phonology: Vol. 1. Production* (pp. 113–142). New York: Academic Press.

Lilez, B. Z. (1985). Cohesion in the narratives of normal and language-disordered children. *Journal of Speech and Hearing Research, 28*, 123–133.

Limber, J. (1973). The genesis of complex sentences. In T. E. Moore (Ed.), *Cognitive development and the acquisition of language* (pp. 169–186). New York: Academic Press.

Locke, J. (1964). *An essay concerning human understanding.* Cleveland: Meridian Books. (Original work published 1690)

Lust, B. (1981). Constraints on anaphora in child language: A prediction for a universal. In S. Tavakolian (Ed.), *Language acquisition and linguistic theory* (pp. 74–96). Cambridge, MA: MIT Press.

Lust, B., & Clifford, T. (1986). The 3-D study: Effects of depth, distance and directionality on children's acquisition of anaphora. In B. Lust (Ed.), *Studies in the acquisition of anaphora: Vol. 1. Defining the constraints* (pp. 203–244). Boston: Reidel.

Lust, B., Solan, L., Flynn, S., Cross, C., & Schuetz, E. (1986). A comparison of null and pronominal anaphora in first language acquisition. In B. Lust (Ed.), *Studies in the acquisition of anaphora: Vol. 1. Defining the constraints* (pp. 245–277). Boston: Reidel.

Macken, M. A. (1980). Aspects of the acquisition of stop systems: A cross-linguistic perspective. In G. H. Yeni-Komshian, J. F. Kavanagh, & C. A. Ferguson (Eds.), *Child phonology: Vol. 1. Production* (pp. 143–168). New York: Academic Press.

MacWhinney, B. (1991). *The CHILDES project: Tools for analyzing talk.* Hillsdale, NJ: Erlbaum.

MacWhinney, B., & Snow, C. (1985). The Child Language Data Exchange System. *Journal of Child Language, 12,* 271–296.

MacWhinney, B., & Snow, C. (1990). The Child Language Data Exchange System: An update. *Journal of Child Language, 17,* 457–472.

Mann, V. A. (1984). Longitudinal prediction and prevention of early reading difficulty. *Annals of Dyslexia, 34,* 117–136.

Mann, V. A. (1986). Why some children encounter reading problems: The contribution of difficulties with language processing and phonological sophistication to early reading disability. In J. K. Torgesen & B. Y. L. Wong (Eds.), *Psychological and educational perspectives on learning disabilities* (pp. 133–159). Orlando, FL: Academic Press.

Mann, V. A., & Liberman, I. Y. (1984). Phonological awareness and verbal short-term memory: Can they presage early reading problems? *Journal of Learning Disabilities, 17,* 592–599.

Mann, V. A., Liberman, I. Y., & Shankweiler, D. (1980). Children's memory for sentences and word strings in relation to reading ability. *Memory & Cognition, 8,* 329–335.

Maratsos, M. (1973). Preschool children's use of definite and indefinite articles. *Child Development, 45,* 446–455.

Maratsos, M. (1976). *The use of definite and indefinite reference.* Cambridge, England: Cambridge University Press.

Marchman, V., & Bates, E. (1994). Continuity in lexical and morphological development: A test of the critical mass hypothesis. *Journal of Child Language, 21,* 339–366.

Markman, E. M. (1990). Constraints children place on word meanings. *Cognitive Science, 14.* Reprinted in P. Bloom (Ed.), (1994), *Language acquisition: Core readings* (pp. 154–173). Cambridge, MA: MIT Press.

Markman, E. M. (1992). The whole object, taxonomic, and mutual exclusivity assumptions as initial constraints on word meanings. In J. P. Byrnes & S. A. Gelman (Eds.), *Perspectives on language and cognition: Interrelations in development*. Cambridge, England: Cambridge University Press.

Markman, E. M., & Hutchinson, J. E. (1984). Children's sensitivity to constraints on word meaning: Taxonomic vs. thematic relations. *Cognitive Psychology, 16,* 1–27.

Markman, E. M., & Wachtel, G. F. (1988). Children's use of mutual exclusivity to constrain the meanings of words. *Cognitive Psychology, 20,* 121-157.

Marler, P. (1991). The instinct to learn. In S. Carey & R. Gelman (Eds.), *The epigenesis of mind: Essays on biology and cognition*. Hillsdale, NJ: Erlbaum. Reprinted in P. Bloom (Ed.), (1994), *Language acquisition: Core readings* (pp. 591–617). Cambridge, MA: MIT Press.

Mattingly, I. (1972). Reading, the linguistic process, and linguistic awareness. In J. Kavanagh & I. Mattingly (Eds.), *Language by ear and by eye* (pp. 133–147). Cambridge, MA: MIT Press.

Mazurkewich, I., & White, L. (1984). The acquisition of the dative alternation: Unlearning overgeneralizations. *Cognition, 16,* 261–283.

McDaniel, D., & Cairns, H. S. (1990). The child as informant: Eliciting linguistic intuitions from young children. *Journal of Psycholinguistic Research, 19,* 331–344.

McDaniel, D., & Cairns, H. S. (in press). Eliciting grammaticality judgments from children. In D. McDaniel, C. McKee, & H. S. Cairns (Eds.), *Methodology in assessing children's syntax*. Cambridge, MA: MIT Press.

McDaniel, D., Cairns, H. S., & Hsu, J. R. (1990). Binding principles in the grammars of young children. *Language Acquisition: A Journal of Developmental Linguistics, 1,* 121–138.

McDaniel, D., Cairns, H. S., & Hsu, J. R. (1990/1991). Control principles in the grammars of young children. *Language Acquisition: A Journal of Developmental Linguistics, 1,* 297–336.

McDaniel, D., Chiu, B., & Maxfield, T. L. (in press). Parameters for wh– movement types: Evidence from child English. *Natural Language and Linguistic Theory*.

McDaniel, D., & Maxfield, T. L. (1992). Principle B and contrastive stress. *Language Acquisition: A Journal of Developmental Linguistics, 2,* 337–358.

McGarrigle, J., & Donaldson, M. (1974). Conservation accidents. *Cognition, 3,* 341–350.

McKain, K. S., Studdert-Kennedy, M., Spieker, S., & Stern, D. (1983). Infant intermodal speech perception is a left-hemisphere function. *Science, 219,* 1347–1349.

McKee, C. (1992). A comparison of pronouns and anaphors in Italian and English acquisition. *Language Acquisition: A Journal of Developmental Linguistics, 2,* 21–54.

McKee, C., Cripe, J., & Campos, M. (1995). *A study of lexical factors in syntactic development*. Manuscript in preparation.

McKee, C., McDaniel, D., & Snedeker, J. (1994). *Relative clauses produced by English-speaking children*. Unpublished manuscript.

McKee, C., Nicol, J., & McDaniel, D. (1993). Children's application of binding during sentence processing. *Language and Cognitive Processes, 8*, 265–290.

McNeill, D. (1966). Developmental psycholinguistics. In F. Smith & G. A. Miller (Eds.), *The genesis of language*. Cambridge, MA: MIT Press.

McTear, M. F. (1985). *Children's conversation*. Oxford: Blackwell.

McTear, M. F. (1987). Communication failure: A developmental perspective. In R. G. Reilly (Ed.), *Communication failure in dialogue and discourse*. Amsterdam: North-Holland-Elsevier.

Mehler, J. (1963). Some effects of grammatical transformations on the recall of English sentences. *Journal of Verbal Learning and Verbal Behavior, 2*, 340–351.

Mehler, J., Jusczyk, P., Lambertz, G., Halsted, N., Bertoncini, J., & Amiel-Tison, C. (1990). A precursor of language acquisition in young infants. *Cognition, 29*, 143–178.

Meier, T. K. (1981). *The comprehension of hints by normal and learning disabled children*. Unpublished doctoral dissertation, The City University of New York.

Mentis, M., & Thompson, S. A. (1991). Discourse: A means for understanding normal and disordered language. In T. M. Gallagher (Ed.), *Pragmatics of language: Clinical practice issues*. Singular Publishing Group.

Menyuk, P. (1969). *Sentences children use*. Cambridge, MA: MIT Press.

Menyuk, P. (1978). *Language and maturation*. Cambridge, MA: MIT Press.

Menyuk, P. (1981). Language development and reading. In J. Flood (Ed.), *Understanding reading comprehension*. International Reading Association.

Menyuk, P. (1991). Metalinguistic abilities and language disorder. In J. Miller (Ed.), *Research on child language disorders: A decade of progress*. Austin, TX: PRO-ED.

Mervis, C. B. (1987). Child-basic object categories and early lexical development. In U. Neisser (Ed.), *Concepts and conceptual development: Ecological and intellectual factors in categorization* (pp. 201–233). Cambridge, England: Cambridge University Press.

Mervis, C. B. (1990). Operating principles, input, and early lexical development. *Communicazioni Scientifiche di Psicologia Generala, 4*, 31–48.

Mevis, C. B., & Long, L. M. (1987). *Words refer to whole objects: Young children's interpretation of the referent of a novel word*. Paper presented at the biennial meeting of the Society for Research in Child Development, Baltimore.

Miller, G. A. (1962). Some psychological studies of grammar. *American Psychologist, 17*, 748–762.

Miller, G. A. (1965). Some preliminaries to psycholinguistics. *American Psychologist, 17,* 15–20.

Miller, J. F. (1981). *Assessing language production in children: Experimental procedures.* Needham Heights, MA: Allyn & Bacon.

Molfese, D. L. (1973). Cerebral asymmetry in infants, children, and adults: Auditory evoked responses to speech and noise stimuli. *Journal of the Acoustical Society of America, 53,* 363.

Morgan, J. L. (1986). *From simple input to complex grammar.* Cambridge, MA: MIT Press.

Mowrer, O. H. (1954). The psychologist looks at language. *The American Psychologist, 9,* 660–694. Reprinted in L. A. Jakobovits & M. S. Miron (Eds.), (1967), *Readings in the psychology of language.* Englewood Cliffs, NJ: Prentice-Hall.

Naigles, L. G. (1990). Children use syntax to learn verb meanings. *Journal of Child Language, 17,* 357–374.

Nelson, K. (1973). Structure and strategy in learning to talk. *Monograph, Society for Research in Child Development, 38*(No. 149).

Nelson, K. (1986). *Event knowledge: Structure and function in development.* Hillsdale, NJ: Erlbaum.

Nelson, K. (1988). Constraints on word learning? *Cognitive Development, 3,* 221–246.

Nelson, N. W. (1993). *Childhood language disorders in context: Infancy through adolescence.* New York: Macmillan.

Newport, E. L. (1990). Maturational constraints on language learning. *Cognitive Science, 14.* Reprinted in P. Bloom (Ed.), (1994). *Language acquisition: Core readings* (pp. 543–560). Cambridge, MA: MIT Press.

Newport, E. L., & Gleitman, L. R. (1977). Maternal self-repetition and the child's acquisition of language. *Papers and Reports on Child Language Development, 13,* 46–55.

Ochs, E., & Shiefflin, B. (Eds.). (1979). *Developmental pragmatics.* New York: Academic Press.

Ojemann, G. A. (1983). Brain organization for language from the perspective of electrical stimulation mapping. *Behavioral and Brain Sciences, 6,* 189–230.

Oller, D. K. (1980). The emergence of the sounds of speech in infancy. In G. H. Veni-Komshian, J. F. Kavanagh, & C. A. Ferguson (Eds.), *Child Phonology: Vol. 1. Production* (pp. 93–112). New York: Academic Press.

Olson-Fulero, L. (1982). Style and stability in mother conversational behavior: A study of individual differences. *Journal of Child Language, 9,* 543–564.

Otsu, Y. (1981). *Universal grammar and syntactic development in children: Toward a theory of syntactic development.* Unpublished doctoral dissertation, Massachusetts Institute of Technology, Cambridge.

Peters, A. M., & Zaidel, E. (1980). The acquisition of homonymy. *Cognition, 8,* 187–207.

Petitto, L. A. (1992). Modularity and constraints in early lexical acquisition: Evidence from children's early language and gesture. In *Minnesota Symposium on Child Psychology, 25.* Reprinted in P. Bloom (Ed.), (1994), *Language acquisition: Core readings* (pp. 95–126). Cambridge, MA: MIT Press.

Philip, B., & Aurelio, S. (1990). Quantifier spreading: Pilot study of preschooler's "every." In T. L. Maxfield & B. Plunkett (Eds.), *University of Massachusetts Occasional Papers: Papers in the Acquisition of WH,* pp. 267–282.

Piaget, J. (1952). *The origins of intelligence in children.* New York: International University Press.

Pinker, S. (1984). *Language learnability and language development.* Cambridge, MA: Harvard University Press.

Pinker, S. (1991). *Learnability and cognition: The acquisition of argument structure.* Cambridge, MA: MIT Press (Bradford).

Pinker, S., & Bloom, P. (1990). Natural language and natural selection. *Behavioral and Brain Sciences, 13,* 707–784.

Pinker, S., Lebeaux, D. S., & Frost, L. A. (1987). Productivity and constraints on the acquisition of the passive. *Cognition, 26,* 195–267.

Poeppel, D., & Wexler, K. (1993). The full competence hypothesis of clause structure in early German. *Language, 69,* 1–33.

Poizner, H., Klima, E. S., & Bellugi, U. (1987). *What the hands reveal about the brain.* Cambridge, MA: MIT Press/Bradford.

Premack, D. (1976). *Intelligence in ape and man.* Hillsdale, NJ: Erlbaum.

Quine, W. V. O. (1960). *Word and object.* Cambridge, MA: MIT Press.

Radford, A. (1990). *Syntactic theory and the acquisition of English syntax: The nature of early child grammars of English.* Oxford: Basil Blackwell.

Rappaport, M., & Levin, B. (1985). *A case study in lexical analysis: The locative alternation.* Unpublished manuscript, MIT Center for Cognitive Science, Cambridge, MA.

Rappaport, M., & Levin, B. (1988). What to do with theta-roles. In W. Wilkins (Ed.), *Thematic relations.* New York: Academic Press.

Reeder, K. (1980). The emergence of illocutionary skills. *Journal of Child Language, 7,* 13–28.

Reinhart, T. (1976). *The syntactic domain of anaphora.* Unpublished doctoral dissertation, Massachusetts Institute of Technology, Cambridge.

Rice, M. L., & Wexler, K. (in press). A phenotype of specific language impairment: Extended optional infinitives. In M. Rice (Ed.), *Toward a genetics of language.* Hillsdale, NJ: Erlbaum.

Roeper, T., & de Villiers, J. (1990). The emergence of bound variable structures. In T. L. Maxfield & B. Plunkett (Eds.), *University of Massachusetts Occasional Papers: Papers in the Acquisition of WH*, pp. 225–266.

Roeper, T., & de Villiers, J. (1992). Ordered decisions and the acquisition of wh–questions. In J. Weissenborn, H. Goodluck, & T. Roeper (Eds.), *Theoretical issues in language acquisition: Papers from the Berlin conference*. Hillsdale, NJ: Erlbaum.

Rosch, E. (1978). Principles of categorization. In E. Rosch & B. Lloyd (Eds.), *Cognition and categorization*. Hillsdale, NJ: Erlbaum.

Rosenbaum, P. (1965). *A principle governing deletion in English sentential complementation*. (Research Paper RC-1519). New York: IBM Watson Research Center.

Ross, J. R. (1967). On the cyclic nature of English pronominalization. In *To Honor Roman Jakobson*. The Hague: Mouton.

Roth, F. (1979). *Effects of intervention on relative clause sentence processing in young normal children*. Unpublished doctoral dissertation, City University of New York.

Roth, F. (1984). Accelerating language learning in young children. *Journal of Child Language, 11*, 89–108.

Russell, B. (1948). *Human knowledge: Its scope and limits*. New York: Simon & Schuster.

Sachs, J., Bard, B., & Johnson, M. L. (1981). Language learning with restricted input: Case studies of two hearing children of deaf parents. *Journal of Applied Psycholinguistics, 2*, 33–54.

Sapir, E. (1933). The psychological reality of phonemes. In D. Mandelbaum (Ed.), (1949), *Selected writings of Edward Sapir*. Berkeley: University of California Press.

Savin, H. B., & Perchonock, E. (1965). Grammatical structure and the immediate recall of English sentences. *Journal of Verbal Learning and Verbal Behavior, 4*, 348–353.

Scarborough, H. S. (1990). Very early language deficits in dyslexic children. *Child Development, 61*, 1728–1743.

Scarborough, H. S. (1991). Early syntactic development of dyslexic children. *Annals of Dyslexia, 41*, 207–220.

Scarborough, H. S., & Dobrich, W. (1990). Development of children with early language delay. *Journal of Speech and Hearing Research, 33*, 70–83.

Schlisselberg, G. (1988). *Development of selected conservation skills and the ability to judge sentential well-formedness in young children*. Unpublished doctoral dissertation, City University of New York.

Schlisselberg, G., & Cairns, H. S. (1995). *Eliciting conservation behavior and form-based grammaticality judgments from young children*. Manuscript in preparation.

Scholl, D. M., & Ryan, E. B. (1980). Development of metalinguistic performance in the early school years. *Language and Speech, 23,* 199–212.

Schwartz, R. (in press). *Language disorders of children.* Austin, TX: PRO-ED.

Searle, J. (1969). *Speech acts.* Cambridge, England: Cambridge University Press.

Seliger, H. W., Krashen, S. D., & Ladefoged, P. (1975). Maturational constraints on acquisition of second-language accents. *Language Sciences, 36,* 20–22.

Shankweiler, D., Crain, S., Brady, S., & Macaruso, P. (1992). Identifying the causes of reading disability. In P. B. Gough, L. C. Ehri, & R. Tresman (Eds.), *Reading acquisition* (pp. 275–305). Hillsdale, NJ: Erlbaum.

Shankweiler, D., & Katz, L. (1994, January). *Dissociation of phonological and syntactic abilities in children with reading disability.* Paper presented at the Boston University Conference on Language Development.

Shapiro, L. P., & Hudson, J. A. (1991). Tell me a make-believe story: Coherence and cohesion in young children's picture-elicited narratives. *Developmental Psychology, 17,* 960–974.

Shatz, M. (1978). Children's comprehension of their mothers' question-directives. *Journal of Child Language, 5,* 39–46.

Shatz, M. (1983). On transition, continuity, and coupling: An alternative approach to communicative development. In R. M. Golinkoff (Ed.), *The transition from prelinguistic to linguistic communication* (pp. 43–55). Hillsdale, NJ: Erlbaum.

Shatz, M., & Gelman, R. (1973). The development of communication skills: Modifications in the speech of young children as a function of the listener. *Monograph, Society for Research in Child Development, 38*(No. 152).

Sheldon, A. (1974). The role of parallel function in the acquisition of relative clauses in English. *Journal of Verbal Learning and Verbal Behavior, 13,* 272–281.

Sherman, J., & Lust, B. (1992). Children are in control. *Cognition, 46,* 1–51.

Shipley, E. F., Smith, C. S., & Gleitman, L. R. (1969). A study in the acquisition of language: Free responses to commands. *Language, 45,* 322–342.

Shultz, T., & Pilon, R. (1973). Development of the ability to detect linguistic ambiguity. *Child Development, 44,* 728–733.

Siple, P. (Ed.). (1978). *Understanding language through sign language research.* New York: Academic Press.

Skinner, B. F. (1957). *Verbal behavior.* New York: Appleton-Century-Crofts.

Skinner, B. F. (1973). *Beyond freedom and dignity.* New York: Knopf.

Slobin, D. I. (1973). Cognitive prerequisites for the development of grammar. In C. A. Ferguson & D. I. Slobin (Eds.), *Studies of child language development* (pp. 175–276). New York: Holt, Rinehart & Winston.

Slobin, D. I. (1985). Crosslinguistic evidence for the language-making capacity. *The crosslinguistic study of language acquisition: Vol. 2. Theoretical issues* (pp. 1157–1256). Hillsdale, NJ: Erlbaum.

Smith, S., Macaruso, P., Shankweiler, D., & Crain, S. (1989). Syntactic comprehension in young poor readers. *Applied Psycholinguistics, 10*, 429–545.

Smith, S., Mann, V. A., & Shankweiler, D. (1986). Spoken sentence comprehension by good and poor readers: A study with the Token Test. *Cortex, 22*, 627–632.

Smith-Lock, K. M. (1993). Morphological analysis and the acquisition of morphology and syntax in specifically language-impaired children. *Haskins Laboratories Status Report on Speech Research*, SR-114, 1–26.

Snow, C. E. (1977). Mothers' speech research: From input to interaction. In C. E. Snow & C. A. Ferguson (Eds.), *Talking to children* (pp. 31–49). Cambridge, England: Cambridge University Press.

Solan, L. (1983). *Prenominal reference: Child language and the theory of grammar.* Boston: Reidel.

Solan, L. (1987). Parameter setting and the development of pronouns and reflexives. In T. Roeper & E. Williams (Eds.), *Parameter setting* (pp. 189–210). Boston: Reidel.

Spelke, E. S. (1988). The origins of physical knowledge. In L. Weiskrantz (Ed.), *Thought without language* (pp. 168–184). Clarendon Press.

Spelke, E., & Cortelyou, A. (1981). In M. E. Lamb & L. R. Sherrod (Eds.), *Infant social cognition: Empirical and theoretical considerations.* Hillsdale, NJ: Erlbaum.

Sperber, D., & Wilson, D. (1986). *Relevance.* Cambridge, MA: Harvard University Press.

Sperber, D., & Wilson, D. (1987). Precis of relevance: Communication and cognition. *Behavioral and Brain Sciences, 10*, 697–754.

Stark, R. E. (1980). Stages of speech development in the first year of life. In G. H. Yeni-Komshian, J. F. Kavanagh, & C. A. Ferguson (Eds.), *Child phonology: Vol. 1. Production* (pp. 73–92). New York: Academic Press.

Stein, C. L., Cairns, H. S., & Zurif, E. B. (1985). Sentence comprehension limitations related to syntactic deficits in reading-disabled children. *Applied Psycholinguistics, 5*(4), 305–322.

Stern, D., Jaffe, J., Beebe, B., & Bennett, S. L. (1975). Vocalizing in unison and in alternation: Two modes of communication within the mother–infant dyad. In D. Aaronson & R. W. Rieber (Eds.), *Developmental psycholinguistics and communication disorders* (pp. 89–100). New York: New York Academy of Sciences.

Strohner, H., & Nelson, K. (1974). The young child's development of sentence comprehension: Influence of event probability, nonverbal context, syntactic form, and strategies. *Child Development, 45*, 567–576.

Sumby, W. H., & Pollack, I. (1954). Visual contribution to speech intelligibility in noise. *Journal of the Acoustical Society of America, 26*, 212–215.

Swinney, D. (1979). Lexical access during sentence comprehension: (Re)consideration of context effects. *Journal of Verbal Learning and Verbal Behavior, 18*, 645–659.

Swinney, D., & Prather, P. (1990). On the comprehension of lexical ambiguity by young children: Investigations into the development of mental modularity. In D. S. Gorfein (Ed.), *Ambiguity processing*. New York: Springer-Verlag.

Tager-Flusberg, H., & Smith, C. (1980, April). *Metalinguistic awareness in preschool children*. Paper presented at the Conference on the Language of the Young Child: Frontier of Research, Brooklyn College, City University of New York.

Tallal, P., Ross, R., & Curtiss, S. (1989). Familial aggregation in specific language impairment. *Journal of Speech and Hearing Disorders, 54*, 167–173.

Tavakolian, S. L. (1978). Children's comprehension of pronominal subjects and missing subjects in complicated sentences. In H. Goodluck & L. Solan (Eds.), *Papers in the structure and development of language* (Vol. 4, pp. 37–83). Amherst: University of Massachusetts.

Tavakolian, S. L. (1981). The conjoined-clause analysis of relative clauses. In S. L. Tavakolian (Ed.), *Language acquisition and linguistic theory*. Cambridge, MA: MIT Press.

Taylor, M., & Gelman, S. A. (1988). Adjectives and nouns: Children's strategies for learning new words. *Child Development, 89*, 411–419.

Thal, D. J., & Tobias, S. (1992). Communicative gestures in children with delayed onset of oral expressive vocabulary. *Journal of Speech and Hearing Research, 35*, 1281–1289.

Tomblin, J. B. (1989). Familial concentration of developmental language impairment. *Journal of Speech and Hearing Disorders, 54*, 287–295.

Tomblin, J. B. (1993). *The genetic epidemiology of specific language impairment*. Paper presented at Merrill Advanced Studies Conference, Toward a Genetics of Language, University of Kansas, Lawrence.

Tunmer, W. E., & Cole, P. G. (1985). Learning to read: A metalinguistic act. In C. S. Simon (Ed.), *Communication skills and classroom success: Therapy methodologies for language–learning disabled students* (pp. 293–312). San Diego: College-Hill.

Tunmer, W. E., & Herriman, M. L. (1984). The development of metalinguistic awareness: A conceptual overview. In W. E. Tunmer, C. Pratt, & M. L. Herriman (Eds.), *Metalinguistic awareness in children* (pp. 12–35). New York: Springer-Verlag.

Tunmer, W. E., Herriman, M. L., & Nesdale, A. R. (1988). Metalinguistic abilities and beginning reading. *Reading Research Quarterly, 23*(2), 134–158.

Tunmer, W. E., Nesdale, A. R., & Wright, A. D. (1987). Syntactic awareness and reading acquisition. *British Journal of Developmental Psychology, 5*, 25–34.

Umstead, R. S., & Leonard, L. B. (1983). Children's resolution of pronominal reference in text. *First Language, 4*, 73–84.

Utakis, S. (1995). *Quantification and definiteness in child grammar*. Unpublished doctoral dissertation, City University of New York.

Valian, V. (1990). Null subjects: A problem for parameter-setting models of language acquisition. *Cognition, 35,* 105–122.

Valian, V. (1991). Syntactic subjects in the early speech of American and Italian children. *Cognition, 40,* 21–81.

Valian, V., Winzemer, J., & Erreich, A. (1981). A "little linguist" model of syntax learning. In S. L. Tavakolian (Ed.), *Language acquisition and linguistic theory.* Cambridge, MA: MIT Press.

van Kleeck, A. (1982). The emergence of linguistic awareness: A cognitive framework. *Merrill-Palmer Quarterly, 28,* 237–265.

Vellutino, F. R. (1979). *Dyslexia: Theory and research.* Cambridge, MA: MIT Press.

Vellutino, F. R. (1987). Dyslexia. *Scientific American, 256,* 34–41.

von Frisch, K. (1953). *The dancing bees: An account of the life and senses of the honey bee* (D. Ilse, Trans.). New York: Harcourt, Brace.

von Frisch, K. (1962). Dialects in the language of the bees. *Scientific American, 207,* 78–87.

Wales, R. (1986). Deixis. In P. Fletcher & M. Garman (Eds.), *Language acquisition* (2nd ed., pp. 401–428). Cambridge, England: Cambridge University Press.

Waltzman, D. (1994). *Principles of binding and control in the grammars of good and poor readers.* Unpublished doctoral dissertation, City University of New York.

Waltzman, D., & Cairns, H. S. (1995). *Principles of binding and control in third grade children.* Manuscript in preparation.

Wankoff, L. S. (1983). *Selected metalinguistic variables as they relate to conservation and reading achievement in normally-achieving and some learning-disabled children.* Unpublished doctoral dissertation, City University of New York.

Wankoff, L. S., & Cairns, H. S. (1983). *Sentential ambiguity detection and its relation to conservation skill.* Unpublished manuscript.

Watkins, R. V., Rice, M. L., & Moltz, C. C. (1993). Verb use by language-impaired and normally developing children. *First Language, 13,* 133–143.

Weinberg, A. (1990). Markedness versus maturation: The case of subject–auxiliary inversion. *Language Acquisition: A Journal of Developmental Linguistics, 1,* 165–195.

Werker, J. F., & Lalonde, C. E. (1988). The development of speech perception: Initial capabilities and the emergence of phonemic categories. *Developmental Psychology, 24,* 672–683.

Wexler, K. (1994). Optional infinitives, head movement and the economy of derivations. In N. Hornstein & D. Lightfoot (Eds.), *Verb movement.* Cambridge, England: Cambridge University Press.

Wexler, K., & Chien, Y-C. (1985). The development of lexical anaphors and pronouns. *Papers and Reports on Child Language Development, 24,* 138–149.

Index

About the Author

Helen Smith Cairns is Professor of Communication Arts and Sciences at Queens College of the City University of New York (CUNY) and is a member of the doctoral faculties in Linguistics and in Speech and Hearing Sciences at the CUNY Graduate School. She earned her Ph.D. from the University of Texas at Austin in 1970 in the field of experimental psychology, with a specialty in psycholinguistics. She joined the faculty of Queens College in 1971, where she has served as Chair of the Department of Communication Arts and Sciences and as Dean of Graduate Studies and Research. Professor Cairns's primary research area is language acquisition in children; she has published widely in this area, as well as in adult psycholinguistics. She is author (with Charles Cairns) of *Psycholinguistics: A Cognitive View of Language* and coeditor (with Dana McDaniel and Cecile McKee) of the forthcoming *Methodology in Assessing Children's Syntax*.